GUIDING GOD'S PEOPLE IN A CHANGING WORLD

A HANDBOOK FOR ELDERS

BY LOUIS M. TAMMINGA

CRC PUBLICATIONS
GRAND RAPIDS, MICHIGAN

Guiding God's People in a Changing World: A Handbook for Elders, © 1998, CRC Publications, 2850 Kalamazoo Ave. SE, Grand Rapids, MI 49560.

Library of Congress Cataloging-in-Publication Data
Tamminga, Louis M., 1930-
    Guiding God's people in a changing world: a handbook for elders / Louis M. Tamminga.
        p.   cm.
    Includes bibliographical references and index.
    ISBN 1-56212-341-6
    1. Christian Reformed Church—Government—Handbooks, manuals, etc.
2. Elders (Church officers)—Handbooks, manuals, etc. I. Title.
BX6826.T36   1998
262'.145731—dc21   98-13269
                                         CIP

10 9 8 7 6 5 4 3 2 1

To Jean,

my partner in ministry

CONTENTS

PREFACE

This book is about elders and for elders. It reflects many years of working side-by-side with elders, not only as a pastor but also as an elder. The settings varied: visits, meetings, shared rides, workshops, seminars, retreats, and more. Perhaps you will recognize on these pages something of the common concerns that elders share.

It is a how-to book of sorts. But I hope that you will find it more than that. The apostle Paul wrote, "Here is a trustworthy saying: If anyone sets his heart on being an overseer [or elder], he desires a noble task" (1 Tim. 3:1). When you were elected and ordained to be an elder in your church, you probably felt more trepidation than Paul seems to admit. But if this handbook will help you to fulfill this noble task more effectively, both the church and you yourself will be the richer for it. And in the end may God receive your thanks for having called you to serve him in this special office.

The book is in five parts. Part One provides a brief biblical background to the office to which you have been called. It probes the tasks of the earliest elders and reveals the similarities to today.

Part Two focuses on you, the person who has accepted God's call to serve as elder. It discusses the nature of calling, how you can prepare yourself for the tasks ahead, what gifts are needed, how you can increase your skills, and so on.

Part Three considers your ministry to individual members entrusted to your care.

Part Four explores the ministry of the consistory and council as they serve the congregation and oversee the programmatic part of church life.

Part Five consists of a brief survey of your church as part of Christian presences beyond the contours of denominational life.

You may read this book to sharpen your skills as an elder or you may consult certain chapters as needs arise in your work. (The Topical Index in the back will serve as a useful guide.) This book can also be used for group study in council meetings, elders' conferences, or training sessions for new elders.

I consulted a variety of source materials, but one book was of particular value to me—*The Manual of Christian Reformed Church Government, 1994 Revision,* by Richard R. De Ridder and Leonard J. Hofman (Grand Rapids, Mich.: CRC Publications, 1998). The *Manual* is the source for many of the references to synodical advice and decisions on the following pages.

—*Louis M. Tamminga*
Grand Rapids, Michigan

1

THE ELDER IN BIBLE TIMES

In Part One of this book we will trace the origins of the office of elder. There are many references to elders both in the Old and New Testaments.

We will see what the Scriptures tell us about the elders' leadership tasks in those early days. We will also examine some examples of their activities. You will find it encouraging to know that you hold a venerable office to which God appended his special promises when he entrusted it to you.

LEADERS AMONG GOD'S ANCIENT PEOPLE

The earliest references in the Bible to elders are found in the book of Exodus. When Israel was a small, struggling nation, held in slavery in Egypt, God placed elders—leaders of families and tribes—among the people. The Bible does not indicate if they held an office, but we do know that Moses relied on their wisdom and understanding. For example, he sought their advice before going to Pharaoh to negotiate the Israelites' exodus from Egypt (Ex. 4:29). That was some three thousand five hundred years ago.

Elders in the Old Testament were leaders among God's people in good times and bad. They were not afraid to take risks. They accompanied Moses on his repeated trips to Pharaoh. They helped Moses lead Israel through desert wanderings to the Promised Land. As the years went by, Moses increasingly depended on their help. Gradually they assumed differing kinds of responsibilities:

- From the community of elders in Israel, Moses appointed some to be rulers in Israel (Ex. 18:24-25).
- He selected seventy elders who accompanied him on special missions (Ex. 24:1-11; Num. 11:16).
- Elders were appointed as judges to dispense justice, sometimes in very complex situations (Deut. 21:1-9).

Later they heard civil cases as they sat in the city gate (Josh. 20:4).
- They were liturgical leaders (Deut. 31:9).
- They were called upon to enforce the law (Deut. 27:1).
- They helped the people by settling disputes (Deut. 25:7-10).
- Some were called to participate in ceremonies celebrating the forgiveness of sins (Lev. 4:15).

During the chaotic years of the judges, the elders were the last resort of reason, protection, and stability for many people. And their absence from the city gate when their services were most needed is a chilling judgment on the city of Jerusalem (Lam. 5:14). At the time of Jesus' birth, elders occupied a prominent place in the religious world, but they missed their finest hour when not one of them had the spiritual foresight to celebrate his coming.

So there you have it: you stand in the tradition of a splendid office exercised by officebearers often excelling, often failing. Although times have changed, you have this in common with your colleagues of ancient Israel—you serve God's people!

THE ELDER IN BIBLE TIMES

The task was not easy then; it is no easier now. Elders failed then; they fail now. God, nevertheless, used them then and continues to use them today. The elders of the Old Testament served the nation of Israel with messianic hope. Elders today serve the church with the hope that the Messiah may be magnified in the lives of his own.

2

CHRIST'S GIFT TO THE NEW TESTAMENT CHURCH

Origin

As is true in the Old Testament, the New Testament gives little detail concerning how the office of elder was instituted. The book of Acts simply reports that there were elders in the local churches. The church in Jerusalem was likely the first to have elders. When there was a famine in that part of the world, Barnabas and Saul delivered aid from the churches in the outlying regions into the hands of the elders at Jerusalem (Acts 11).

Soon after, perhaps inspired by this good provision in the church of Jerusalem, Paul and Barnabas "appointed elders for them in each church" (Acts 14:23). Later Paul instructed Titus to "appoint elders in every town" (Titus 1:5). These appointments had a deeper dimension. Paul pointed out later that the offices were a gift from Christ to the churches (Eph. 4:11-16). Elders today also assume their office by divine appointment.

Responsibility

The Bible describes the wide variety of tasks performed by New Testament elders. For example:

- When problems arose—as they always do when churches grow—the elders searched the will of God for solutions (Acts 15:5-6).

- They assisted the apostles—who had the unique task of laying the foundation of the New Testament church—and consoled them with tears of empathy (Acts 20:37).
- They ordained gifted church workers to offices connected with specific tasks (1 Tim. 4:14).
- They "directed the affairs" of the churches (1 Tim. 5:17).
- They prayed with parishioners for healing (James 5:14).
- They preached and taught (1 Tim. 5:17).

In Revelation the apostle John hints at the glory of the church by mentioning twelve times the elders among the believers.

Names

In the original Greek two words are translated "elder": *presbuteros* and *episcopos*. *Presbuteros*, from which we have the word "presbyter," refers to an older person who by reason of age has acquired wisdom. *Episcopos*, or "bishop," refers to the elder's function as an overseer of God's people.

Another common designation is "shepherd." Both Paul and Peter urged the elders to be shepherds. Paul said the elders are to "be shepherds of the church of God" (Acts 20:28). And Peter

urged the elders to be "shepherds of
God's flock" (1 Pet. 5:2).

You are called by God to be a shepherd
to his flock. The responsibilities and
tasks of that calling will fill the rest of
this book.

PART 2

THE WELL-EQUIPPED SERVANT

Part Two focuses on you, the person who has accepted the office of elder. We will discuss the nature of calling, how you can prepare yourself for the tasks ahead, what gifts are needed, and how you can increase your skills.

THE NATURE OF DIVINE CALLING

Elders, though chosen by members of the local church, are called and appointed to their office by God himself. The Christian Reformed form for the Ordination of Elders and Deacons repeatedly mentions this divine appointment, making reference to the three persons of the Trinity:

The Father
"God our heavenly Father, who has called you to these sacred offices ..."

"Our merciful Father in heaven, we thank you that you have provided ... elders ..."

The Son
"As the Lord of the church he appoints leaders ..."

"I charge you, people of God, to receive these officebearers as Christ's gift to the church."

The Holy Spirit
"... and by his Spirit equips them ..."

"I charge you elders to 'guard yourselves and all the flock of which the Holy Spirit has made you overseers.'"

The form drives the point home with this personal question to you: "Do you believe that in the call of the congregation God himself is calling you to these holy offices?" The Christian Reformed Synod underscored the importance of this call when it declared: "Officebearers are elected and called by the congregation, in which process those chosen must acknowledge the call of Jesus Christ" (*Acts of Synod 1987*, pp. 393-394).

As you perform your duties, remind yourself again and again of the reality that your mandate is from heaven!

What are the implications of this divine appointment? Of course, there is no mystery about it. You will not suddenly find yourself endowed with all kinds of new gifts and skills. Parishioners won't always agree with your decisions. Relationships may sometimes be strained.

However, divine appointment will enable you to deal confidently with unsettling doubts about your eldership. If your appointment had been a matter between you and those who voted you in, then you would be no more than a board member of a society. But God always casts the deciding ballot in the voting process. You serve because God called you to serve. You still have your human limitations—you may not be the best speaker, you may be shy, you may be inept at times, you may make mistakes—but you must not entertain the defeatist notion, "Others can do this better than I."

You and your God are in this assignment together!

Divine appointment has yet another aspect. When you were (or will be) ordained to office, the minister addressed the congregation with these words: "I charge you, people of God, to receive these officebearers as Christ's gift to the church. . . . Hold them in honor; take their counsel seriously. . . ." Those are true and reassuring words. Relationships may not always be healthy in your church. There may even be hard feelings at times, but both you and the congregation know that the office of elder is God-given and is, therefore, to be held in high regard.

THE ELDER—A PERSON OF GIFTS

You have gifts and abilities, skills and talents. Your council recognized them when they nominated you for office and submitted your name to the congregation. The congregation recognized your gifts too, and has indicated that they want you to use them in service.

Although you are, indeed, gifted to serve, you may not have all the gifts needed for effective leadership in your congregation. Other officebearers, however, possess gifts that you do not have. As gifted elders, you complement each other. Your consistory and council will be most effective when you and your colleagues use your individual gifts for the good of the whole.

While not every elder has every gift, the form for Ordination of Elders and Deacons mentions a number of gifts that every elder should possess in some measure. These include

Christlikeness. You may not think of yourself as particularly Christlike. You may feel that you have some growing to do, but when you take your sins to the Savior's cross and cast your lot with him, you are Christlike.

Maturity in the faith. A crop matures at the end of a full season of growth. Similarly, elders must be "seasoned," or tested, in the faith. That seasoning may include enduring difficult situations, being faithful at a price, exercising consistent diligence, and overcoming temptations (Heb. 13:6-8). As an elder maturing in the faith, you will have the patience to reason with unreasonable people. In trying and complex situations you will not become upset quickly nor be offended easily. And you will go for substance rather than for show.

Prayer. Prayer is the privilege of all believers, but prayer is the special gift of elders. David, for example, was a self-described "man of prayer" (Ps. 109:4). In the same sense, the form calls elders to be people of prayer. It's a gift that one cultivates by faithful obedience.

Patience. This gift does not come easily for most people. It clashes with our natural inclination to take action and to take it now. Patience is the slow-growing fruit of waiting with trust. The Latin word from which *patience* has been derived means "pain." How true! Patience can be painful.

Humility. Most Christian graces are hard to come by. Humility is one of them. The word *humility* comes from a Latin word that means "to be close to the ground." You get the idea. Some of your people have been beaten down by life. They are, as it were, lying on the ground. You, in turn, must get down on their level to make eye contact. Humility is the true spirit of leadership (Matt. 20:26-28).

The form also includes a prayer for two other important gifts: enthusiasm and a sense of sustained awe.

Enthusiasm literally means "God-indwelled." By meditating on God's Word and allowing him to indwell our inner beings, we become enthused people. We also are "God-indwelled" because God is present in the church through the Holy Spirit. The indwelling of the Holy Spirit is God's greatest gift to us. The Spirit gives you, the office-bearer, the power to express the gifts Christ has entrusted to you.

Awe, says the dictionary, stems from a mixture of reverence, fear, and wonder, caused by something majestic and sublime. *Awe* and *enthusiasm* are closely related. Aren't those the feelings you get when you see the great works of God among his people? You cannot effectively do the work of an elder if you don't know a sense of awe. Without it the holy things of God tend to become commonplace. (For a study of other characteristics of elders, see Gal. 5:22-23; 1 Tim. 3:1-7; Titus 1:6-9; 1 Pet. 5:1-4.)

The form for the Ordination of Elders and Deacons mentions one more gift, seemingly in passing, in the charge to the elders. Elders are to be wise counselors. Wisdom is a gift so foundational that it deserves a section of its own.

THE GIFT AND PRACTICE OF WISDOM

Wisdom is a lamp that illumines all the other gifts. Some say that wisdom cannot be learned. You either have it or you don't, they insist. There is probably some truth to that. Sadly, some people lack wisdom even in old age. I believe that wisdom can grow and perhaps even flourish in a person's life.

Solomon prayed for wisdom, and God granted his request (1 Kings 3:9-12). The apostle James advises all believers to ask God for wisdom (James 1:5) with the firm assurance that he will respond favorably to such prayers.

A special kind of seeing

"Wisdom" comes from the Latin word *videre,* or "to see." Seeing is an important component of wisdom. You, the wise elder, see situations as they truly are. You see them from all sides. You consider them with clarity. You see them in their correct proportion. You see them in their relation to broader realities. You see their causal connections. You perceive the probable outcome of their interactions.

Seeing has another dimension. Wisdom allows you to see yourself as you truly are: your ideals, prejudices, hopes, memories, experiences, weaknesses, strengths, interests, misgivings, anger, fears, and so on. You become aware that all these factors affect your relationships with your people. An unwise elder, for example, may inadvertently bring some personal "garbage" to an encounter with a parishioner.

A special kind of doing

You can train yourself to practice seeing through the lens of wisdom. In doing so, you will create a climate in which wisdom can flourish. Here are some ideas to get you started:

1. Don't rush. Give yourself some time before you make a decision or give advice in difficult situations. Sleep on it. Pray about it. Even then, if possible, live a few days with your intended advice or decision before you make it known.

2. Be comprehensive in your assessment of situations. Have you considered all the facts? Do you understand the background of the events? Are you driven by a true desire to serve? Have you heard from all the parties involved? Have you sought good advice? Check your motives. Be a sympathetic player in the drama. Check your own fears. Acknowledge that it is sometimes hard to be totally honest with yourself.

3. Don't be a loner. Wisdom flourishes best when counsel is taken communally. Seek the advice of your colleagues in office. Learn from them. Listen hard to those whose viewpoint differs from yours. Welcome and grow from encounters that "stretch" you.

4. Be a constructive ponderer. It is not helpful to fret and worry about people and situations all day long. Rather, take some time out, go into your inner room, be alone, and concentrate intentionally on the matter at hand. Talk with yourself. Reason and argue with yourself. Keep at it. Make notes. Weave prayers into such moments. By doing so you will gain an accurate and helpful perspective on the situation you face. The course you choose will probably be illumined by wisdom.

5. Maintain your focus. Church life can be confusing. As an elder you have a lot on your mind. Remind yourself to stay the course. Focus on the greater goal of church life. Focus on the ideals you have set for your work as an elder. Bring your inner resources to bear on the ultimate goal. The focused elder is likely to do his work with wisdom.[1]

Note

1. See also *Our World Belongs to God—A Contemporary Testimony* (Grand Rapids, Mich.: CRC Publications, 1986), sec. 37-39.

DEVELOPING KNOWLEDGE AND SKILLS

It goes without saying that shepherding God's flock will require a good deal of your time. You should also expect to set aside time for training and study. Take advantage of opportunities to increase your knowledge and skill. In the long run you will be glad you did. By gaining knowledge and skill you will do a better job of serving the church. Here are some practical things you can do:

- Read the confessions of the church and the church order.
- Attend elders' conferences and workshops. They will prepare you for service and enrich you personally.
- If you are a new elder, make an appointment to sit down with an experienced elder and talk things over. You can learn a lot by doing so, and the fellowship will be valuable.

- Your council would do well to set aside time in the agenda for studying a topic related to your work. Sometimes the pastor takes the initiative to arrange the discussion. Such study is a nurturing experience for all office-bearers.[1]

Note

1. For further help see Neil de Koning, *Guiding the Faith Journey* (Grand Rapids, Mich.: CRC Publications, 1996), pp. 7-31.

ONGOING DEPENDENCE ON THE BIBLE

It's obvious, isn't it? All Christians should read the Bible, and elders should set the example. I know from personal experience, and you do probably too, that it takes some doing to be a serious Bible reader.

Regular Bible reading brings two rewards to the elder. The form for Ordination of Elders and Deacons hints at the first one: the Bible is the source from which you draw to minister to the members entrusted to your care. The form advises you to "know the scriptures," which are "useful for teaching, rebuking, correcting, and training in righteousness" (2 Tim. 3:16). As you perform your tasks in the church, make mental notes of needs, challenges, problems, and struggles as you observe them. Then try to determine how the Bible addresses them.

The second benefit of Bible reading has to do with your own spiritual well-being. Life is demanding. Being an elder only adds to the stress. Be serious about replenishment. Your batteries need recharging regularly. If you neglect your-self, you will eventually "burn out." So make Bible reading a regular part of your daily routine.

Perhaps you will find it helpful to conclude your reading with a few moments of silence during which you ponder and pray over the verses you have just read. Then, throughout the day, intentionally try to recall the message that comes to you. It will help you to face the day in God's company and to discern his will.[1]

Joining with other believers in a church-based Bible study will also encourage you. Such groups may be found in most churches. As an elder you will profit from either joining a study group or using your gift of leadership to start one. Surely the group will be encouraged by your presence.

Note

1. See also *Our World Belongs to God*, sec. 34-36.

DEVOTED TO PRAYER

Here is another demand on your time—prayer. Yes, do it! Take time from your crowded schedule to pray.

First, pray for yourself. It will help you to deal with the busyness of your life. Prayer refreshes, replenishes, and strengthens the one who prays. As you exit your prayer closet, you will do so with a new sense of wholeness and enthusiasm for your ministry.

In addition, pray for your people. Prayer for the individuals and families entrusted to your care is not optional. It is a requirement of the office you have accepted. The form for ordination affirms, "officebearers must exercise their office with prayer." In the charge to the elders, you are directed to "pray continually for the church."

Here is an idea to make your prayers more meaningful. Consider making a list of people in your district and adding details about their lives as you observe them. Then pray through the list at regu-

> Prayer is not overcoming God's reluctance. It is laying hold of God's highest willingness.
> —Richard Trench

lar intervals. You will soon find that such prayer is a worthy component of your activities. You will probably also find that prayer will help you to fight against procrastination. So, yes, do place your own name on your prayer list too.

MANAGING YOUR TIME

How can you do it all? Isn't that your experience—so much to do, so little time to do it? Before we settle for that as an intractable reality, however, allow me to make some suggestions.

Time is like water which can, ever so slowly, disappear. However, time, like water, can be managed. Time management can be learned; you can even make it a way of life.

Here is an example. An elder with whom I once served stopped by my office to tell me that he had not visited the people in his district that season. He explained that he had just been too busy. I asked him whether he did any planning and scheduling in his life.

"Not really," he said. I made a proposal to him: "Would you be able to devote one evening every two weeks to visiting?" He thought for a moment and nodded. "Now suppose," I said, "that of the twelve months of the year you would designate eight months for visiting."

"Fair enough," he said. "Well then," I said, "that would give you sixteen evenings during that eight-month season. Suppose you would schedule two visits per evening. That would enable you to make thirty-two visits."

"Amazing," he said. "That's the number of addresses in my district."

Subduing the calendar is, however, only half the battle. Other steps are involved. You may wish to begin by making a survey of your tasks. Settle for what you can do, and then set goals accordingly. Only then can you do your scheduling. Lay out the weeks and months of the church year in blocks on large sheets of paper. Pencil in the stated meetings of the council, consistory, and committees, as far as you know them. Next, mark the evenings you want to set aside for visiting. Make appointments well ahead of time. Keep track of tasks performed and visits made.

I suggest that you discuss this process with your spouse. Mutual agreement on the extent of your involvement is important. If, in the course of the season, you are away from home more than you and your spouse had anticipated, you should review your schedule and make adjustments.

I realize that life's circumstances are unpredictable. Unforeseen events may wreak havoc with your schedule. Don't worry; revisions can be made. Don't hesitate to inform your colleagues when there are some tasks that you simply cannot complete. Perhaps they can come to your aid. As you deal with unexpected timing conflicts, remember that you would be worse off with no schedule. Now you have a means to track and reschedule tasks you could not do. That's one of the advantages of planning. It also shows that you are trying to be a good steward of your time.

FEELING INADEQUATE

All elders feel inadequate at times. There are no simple solutions. Serving the Master doesn't happen without pain and struggle. Remember, sowers often sow in tears (Ps. 126:5).

Consider these suggestions:

* Make sure that you have the right perspective on your role as an elder. You are responsible for ministering to your people. You must do that in the proper spirit of involvement and empathy. You are not responsible for the outcome, however. You minister on Christ's behalf. He gives the increase—in his time and in his way. Don't berate yourself in the seeming absence of success.
* Don't belittle yourself if your work seems to flounder. According to article 2 of the Church Order, your office carries dignity and honor. You are a person of dignity and honor. That may not seem very real to you, but to Christ it is. It would be very encouraging if the members of your district occasionally expressed their appreciation to you in some meaningful way. That happens all too infrequently. Still, you should carry on with the confidence that your flock will keep its promise made at the time of your ordination, that is, to "hold [the new elders] in honor . . . [and to] sustain them in prayer and encourage them . . . especially when they feel the burden of their office."
* The form includes another wonderful promise: "[The Lord] appoints leaders and by his Spirit equips them. . . ." Remember—when you do the best you can do, the Spirit will give the increase. His invisible blessings are often the most enduring ones! Don't neglect to seek out your colleagues in ministry for mutual prayer, consultation, encouragement, and thanksgiving. Officebearers can be each other's greatest encouragers. (See section 48.)

A SPIRITUAL VISION FOR THE CHURCH

In 2 Corinthians 5:20 the apostle Paul states that all believers are called to the ministry of reconciliation. "We are therefore Christ's ambassadors, as though God were making his appeal through us. We implore you on Christ's behalf: Be reconciled to God."

This is Paul's spiritual vision for the church. You as an elder stand in a great apostolic tradition as you lead your congregation toward the same vision. As you think of the people under your care, pray that they themselves will achieve divine reconciliation with God and with each other.

The church has a spiritual purpose that is invisible to the world. To you as an elder, much of it is visible. The ministry of reconciliation is the foundation of your congregation's ministry. As you lead, you must keep that vision "front and center" so that every part of your church's life contributes to the reconciliation God desires.

The form for ordination includes this prayer: "Under [these officebearers'] guidance may your church grow in every

> No one wanted to be considered least. Then Jesus took a towel and a basin and so redefined greatness. —Unknown

spiritual grace, in faith which is open and unashamed. . . ." Keep that vision! Maintain that focus! (See also section 51.)

3

PART 3

MOVING AMONG GOD'S PEOPLE

We now turn our attention to the personal contact you will have with the people of your district. This activity must be viewed in the context of your work as a member of consistory and council. These two areas are closely connected. When you minister to your people, you do so as a consistory member. And, conversely, the work of your consistory and council must always display a deep concern for the welfare of your people.

So while we distinguish between the tasks of personal caregiving and participation in the work of consistory and council, we don't separate them.

Note: In keeping with synodical usage, we refer to "consistory" as the body of elders and minister(s) and to "council" as the body of deacons, elders, and minister(s).

DISTRICTS

The members of most congregations are organized into districts. The district system has several advantages for both member and elder. Having your own district enables you to develop a personal relationship with a limited number of parishioners. For the three years of your term in office, you accompany them on their pilgrimage. You get to know them, you share their sorrows and joys, and you witness their struggles toward growth.

Having a district enables you to bring continuity and consistency to your ministry. Every contact builds on the previous one. You develop mutual trust—one great prerequisite for doing your work effectively.

Some churches have large districts, each served by a team of two elders. Others have smaller districts with one elder in charge. Both have advantages. When you are part of a team, you and your fellow elder can encourage and advise each other. When difficulties develop, you can deliberate together. Between the two of you, accountability will probably develop.

When you serve a district alone, you have fewer people to oversee. You may get to know them better, and it takes less time to make the rounds.

In many congregations a deacon is assigned to each district. This is a commendable arrangement. The district elder and district deacon can function as a team with the understanding that each does the work appropriate to his or her office. The elder and deacon keep each other informed about needs and opportunities they observe. They may plan activities together and go together on an occasional visit when necessary.

Many churches cluster membership activities around the districts, generally with good results. If this describes your church, you may consider appointing a district coordinator to facilitate activities. The elder, deacon, and coordinator may then form a team through which district life can be administered effectively and new initiatives may be given productive expression.

A growing number of churches now encourage members to participate in small groups. In such groups a dozen (or fewer) members meet at regular times to pray, meditate, study, and share mutual concerns. District elders should remain in regular contact with the groups in their districts and visit them as time permits. Small group leaders may be drawn into the district leadership.[1]

Note
1. See also *Home Fellowship Groups* (Grand Rapids, Mich.: CRC Publications) and *Guiding the Faith Journey*, pp. 53-58.

KNOWING YOUR PEOPLE

In order to be a spiritual blessing to your people, you must become acquainted with them. Life for your district members may be a difficult saga in which successes and setbacks are constantly absorbing their attention.

Remember that these life experiences are important to your people. When they have particular problems and personal pain, they will appreciate your concern and empathy. In times of good fortune, they will appreciate your interest.

You may be surprised to know that some of your members are lonely. Through your good care they will experience a taste of the community of believers. This is especially true of the elderly. When your congregation gathers for fellowship activities, seek out individual members and discretely inquire about ongoing developments in their lives. They will deeply appreciate your intelligent concern.

Children and young people need your special attention. Their lives are filled with excitement but also with anxiety. Ordinarily you will need to initiate contact with them. They will not give their trust readily, but if you show consistent, genuine interest in their well-being— usually best expressed in a one-to-one setting—they will open their hearts to you.

Do you size up people and situations correctly? Jesus always saw everything in the right perspective. That was one of the reasons why he was able to fulfill the task God gave him.

The right perspective opens the way toward the right service.

Christ saw the multitude not as a hostile crowd, but as sheep without a shepherd (Matt. 9:36); he saw wastrels not as hopeless cases, but as children whom the Father would welcome home (Luke 15:11-32); he saw outsiders not as people who don't count for much, but as potential Good Samaritans (Luke 10:25-37); he saw the church not as a body that is constantly failing but beautiful as his bride (Rev. 22:17), useful as the salt of the earth (Matt. 5:13) and the light of the world (Matt. 5:14).

His followers can serve best when they have Christ's perspective on people and situations. They can because they have put on the mind of Christ (1 Cor. 2:16).

RECORD KEEPING IS VITAL

Keeping good records of your work as an elder is vitally important. As soon as you are installed in office, set up your personal logbook. Write in it all the basic information for every member in your district: address, phone, age, job, school, skills and gifts, functions in church and beyond, and so on. In the months ahead, remember to record important events in the members' lives and your dealings with them. Record dates and highlights of the visits you have with them. Review your logbook regularly to remain current with the members of your district. Whenever you meet with one of your people, you can then refer to their concerns.

Once your people know that you are sincerely interested in them, they will come to trust you and will more easily contact you when needs arise.

Paging through the logbook I kept as a pastor and later as an elder, I come upon such entries as the following:

John B.: laid off; visited March 3
Mary O.: valedictorian, high school graduation
Beth K.: baby boy John Adam, Nov. 2
Bert P.: left for University of Iowa
Gert A.: transferred to Room 166 at the Manor

Jane E.: would like to play violin in church; told the committee, Apr. 3
Claude VB.: bought new truck
Paul U.: became partner in firm
Helen and Pete D.V.: baby remains colicky; phoned Oct. 10
John B.: job prospects still bleak; phoned March 30
David and Sally L.: 50th wedding anniversary; visited Sept. 13
Mary V.: will be ten next Sunday
Pat and John C.: kitchen fire, July 18
Jack T.: father in Canada died, June 2
Debra S.: discussed problem she had with music c'tee, Feb. 11

My log frequently reminded me of an overdue visit or a phone call that should be made. I found that record keeping does not take much time. It gave me some assurance that I was on top of things pastorally.

When you near the end of your term as an elder, consider making a summary of your log for the benefit of your successor. Be careful to omit confidential information.

FORMING A SPIRITUAL COMMUNITY THROUGH COVENANTAL LIVING

The spiritual life of your congregation has two dimensions. The people grow in their relationship to God and to each other. Through the church's ministry the members increasingly experience the reality of covenantal life: love for God and for their neighbor (Mark 12:30-31).

This dual covenantal vision should mark your service to God's people. This does not suggest that you should always engage in "spiritual talk" when you meet a member of your district. Take advantage of small talk with your parishioners, but always keep their need for spiritual growth in the back of your mind. The apostle Paul said, "We will in all things grow up into him who is the Head, that is, Christ" (Eph. 4:15).

That same covenantal concern helps you see every believer as part of the Christian community. It hurts your elder's heart when members don't feel at home in the congregation, when they feel slighted, or when they are divided over issues and policies. The most common reason why people join a church is because they find meaningful fellowship there. The absence of such fellowship is the most common reason why they leave. The words of Paul quoted above have a sequence: "From him the whole body, joined and held together by every supporting ligament, grows and builds itself

up in love, as each part does its work" (Eph. 4:16). Elders are incurably covenant minded: establish people in God and establish people in community. They have heard the apostle Peter's challenge: "To the elders among you, I appeal as a fellow elder . . . be shepherds of God's flock that is under your care, serving as overseers . . . being examples to the flock" (1 Pet. 5:1-3).

Spiritual development has an additional dimension. Note that Paul teaches that the body "grows and builds itself up in

> Tending relationships marked by integrity, respect, and thoughtfulness becomes a source of replenishment.
>
> As we give, we receive.
>
> Replenishment is then woven into the busy routine of the day.

love, as each part does its work." A spiritual community is endurably successful when the members begin to care for each other. Actually that's how most pastoral work is done in flourishing churches, as members pastor members. Mutual caregiving and care-receiving become a way of life for the congregation.[1]

The apostle John summarized such spiritual growth when he wrote, "Love one another....We know that we have passed from death to life, because we love our brothers. . . . This is how we know what love is: Jesus Christ laid down his life for us. And we ought to lay down our lives for our brothers. If anyone has material possessions and sees his brother in need but has no pity on him, how can the love of God be in him? Dear children, let us not love with words or tongue but with actions and in truth" (1 John 3:11, 14, 16-18). (Note that the word *truth* is related to "troth" and "trust," both key elements in wholesome relationships.)

This is the emphasis of the Church Order, article 79b, where it states: "The consistory shall . . . foster a spirit of love and openness within the fellowship. . . ."[2]

What can you do to promote mutually nurturing relationships?

1. In your contacts with your district members, discern whether each person has an enriching relationship with another member. Challenge your members to encourage and help each other. Perhaps you can ask one member to visit another member who is ill. Or you might direct one member toward another member who has a specific need. Elders, deacons, and ministers may need to cooperate in making these arrangements.

2. In your district's group activities— which you will attend periodically— remind members of the need for mutual care. Invite group participants to express prayer concerns and challenge them to pray for those requests.

3. Most churches now have a telephone prayer chain through which members are informed of needs, joys, and challenges. Your district will benefit from its own prayer chain, but you will need to see that it happens. Sharing items of personal interest will contribute to a sense of intimacy.

4. Churches often publish congregational newsletters and distribute lists of prayer concerns. Encourage your members to use these vehicles to make news and prayer items known to the larger body.

5. Pay close attention to new members, seekers, and inquirers, many of whom may struggle with loneliness and other difficulties. By establishing a trust relationship with them, you may be able to link them up with caring members of your district.

6. Tell your pastor that you would like to assist in establishing nurturing relationships in the church. Encourage your pastor to make this type of spiritual development part of the preaching.[3]

Notes
1. See also *Our World Belongs to God,* sec. 41.
2. See also *Motivating Members for Ministry* (Grand Rapids, Mich.: CRC Publications).
3. See also *Guiding the Faith Journey,* pp. 65-95.

SPIRITUAL FORMATION—
QUEST FOR CERTAINTY AND GODLINESS

You will find that many of your members have two basic concerns: how to experience and live out their salvation, and how to deal with nagging doubt and failures. These are two sides of one coin. Your people have a yearning to live close to God, yet they are often disappointed in themselves. Life comes with so many demands and pressures. They want to experience joy, but they often feel empty and sad.

How can you help your people experience godliness, personal piety, or spiritual formation in their lives?

The Greek word for "godliness" is *eusebeia,* which occurs fifteen times in the New Testament. The New Testament links godliness to the fruit of God's saving grace in believers. Because of Christ's death and resurrection God justified us and declared us to be his children (Rom. 5:1-11; 1 John 3:1). We are saved by faith in Christ. That's the source of our certainty. When we place our trust in personal piety and bank on it for certainty, we are in for disappointment and frustration.

All through history there have been movements that spelled out patterns of piety. This established code of conduct was the condition for belonging to the community. The members showed loyalty to the community, spoke its language, and defended its positions on issues. The community, in turn, afforded the members a sense of belonging, security, self-worth, and, especially, assurance of salvation. Legalism and bondage invariably followed in the wake of such developments.

In your ministry to God's people, hammer home the theme of salvation by grace through faith resulting in lives of service fueled by Spirit-power. (Once biblical assurance of faith has been established and subjective doubt has been addressed, believers are better equipped to live lives of godliness.)

You can do this using the tools for spiritual formation provided by the church. These tools are found in the confessions of the Reformation. You may consider reading Lord's Day 32 of the Heidelberg Catechism and teaching it to your members when you are assembled in a group meeting.

Lord's Day 32 begins with a glorious assumption: "We have been delivered from our misery by God's grace alone through Christ...." That's the foundation! That's the source! Then we have a beautiful conclusion: "We do good because Christ by his Spirit is also renewing us to be like himself, so that in all our living we may show that we are thankful to God for all that he has done for us, and so that he may be praised through us."

But there is more in Lord's Day 32. Once we have grasped the biblical order of things, we discover that good works of piety actually do play a role in deepening our assurance of salvation. The catechism puts it this way: "And we do good so that we may be assured of our faith by its fruits, and so that by our godly living our neighbors may be won over to Christ."

Spiritual formation, then, needs a firm biblical foundation and perspective. Once this is a growing concern among your people, they will be motivated to seek spiritual nurture and discipline: reading Scripture, meditating on Scripture, praying alone and together, talking with God, setting aside time for devotional reading, and participating in retreats and conferences.[1]

Note

1. Resources from CRC Publications to assist with spiritual formation include: Neil de Koning, *Guiding the Faith Journey*, 1996; Alvin J. Vander Griend, *Keys to a Praying Church,* 1996; and Don Postema, *Space for God,* 1983, 1997. Also consult Ben Campbell Johnson, *Speaking of God* (Louisville: Westminster/John Knox Press, 1991), pp. 11-30. For meditation reading: *Today—The Family Altar* (Palos Heights, Ill.: The Back to God Hour).

STEWARDSHIP AS A WAY OF LIFE

Those who walk in the power of God's grace dedicate their lives to his service. They live a life of stewardship. Stewardship springs from the vision that God made us, redeemed us, and provides for us; what we are and what we have we owe to him. In stewardship we dedicate ourselves and our possessions to him.

What does that mean in practice?

Consider the Macedonian Christians. The apostle Paul tells us:

"We want you to know about the grace that God has given the Macedonian churches. Out of the most severe trial, their overflowing joy and their extreme poverty welled up in rich generosity. For I testify that they gave as much as they were able, and even beyond their ability. Entirely on their own, they urgently pleaded with us for the privilege of sharing in this service to the saints" (2 Cor. 8:1-4).

The elders, deacons, and pastor of First CRC met with the finance committee to discuss money matters. "The news is not good," said the spokesperson for the committee. "We are not meeting this year's budget by a long shot. The projected deficit runs into the thousands."

Next came the deacons' report. The secretary handed out sheets containing a long list of causes to which the deacons proposed gifts be sent. The deacons explained that the total of their proposed annual giving to various causes was higher than ever due to increased needs everywhere.

Discussion followed.

Someone suggested that, sad as it was, reality seemed to dictate that the deacons wait with sending the gifts until the budget deficit had been met. Then a deacon said, "Our congregation is not rich, but it is not poor either, and our members are not stingy. Last month we had a special offering for Mrs. K's eye surgery, and we collected twice the amount needed. I propose that we tell the congregation about our dilemma, that money is needed for our vibrant ministry program, but also for the indispensable ministries of these causes. And let us trust that the congregation will respond."

The following Sunday a deacon explained the challenge to the congregation, and the minister shared his vision of stewardship. Later that year a grateful finance committee reported that the budget had been met, and the deacons noted that they had received sufficient funds to cover checks sent to every special cause.

Stewardship had become a way of life for the Macedonian Christians despite their "extreme poverty." We follow their example, for we know that God is the owner. He owns our skills, our ambitions, our things, our many loves. What we own is simply on loan from God. We manage our lives for him. We are his stewards.

Stewards are secure people. They know that the giving of their Father never ceases. He is there for them. And so they go in his name—to the poor who need relief, to the grieving who need solace, to the hungry who need bread, to the lonely who need a friend. They are there when the church needs workers, when campaigns need funds, and when programs need volunteers. Stewardship is a way of life.

What can you do as an elder?

• Practice financial stewardship in your own life. Manage your affairs wisely and responsibly. Be generous in supporting God's work in his world. Make stewardship a spiritual service for yourself. Only then will you have the spiritual courage and freedom to lead your members in their stewardly calling.

• Set forth a clear vision of biblical stewardship in council meetings, with your pastor, and among your members. Stewardship goes far beyond "fund raising." Its first beneficiary is the giver as he or she actively shares in the coming of the kingdom of God on earth. What your members give is determined more by their motivation for giving than by the extent of their resources.[1]

Note

1. For other helpful suggestions see Robert C. Heerspink, *Becoming a Firstfruits Congregation* (Grand Rapids, Mich.: Barnabas Foundation/ CRC Publications/RCA Foundation, 1996).

IN THE WORLD

Your congregation is deeply affected by modern society. No one can fully understand the dynamics of being *in the world,* but not *of the world.* Nevertheless, be aware that society affects your people in at least two ways: it entices them with material rewards, and it frightens them with omens of evil and doom.

This generation witnesses the world passing from one millennium to the next. Will the new century usher in the wilderness age? Will public morality continue to erode and greed become more brazen in high places?

According to *Our World Belongs to God,* sec. 3

"Rebel cries sound through the world:
some, crushed by failure
or hardened by pain,
give up on life and hope and God;
others, shaken,
but still hoping for human triumph,
work feverishly to realize their
   dreams."

These realities especially challenge the church's ministry in two ways.

First, the church must be prophetically faithful. It must seek to instill in the membership a deep sensitivity toward holy living. And it must be God's voice in society,

calling the ruling authorities to champion goodness, decency, and righteousness. Jesus said to his Father in heaven, "I have given them your word and the world has hated them, for they are not of the world any more than I am of the world. My prayer is not that you take them out of the world but that you protect them from the evil one. They are not of the

> I simply argue that the cross of Christ must be raised again in the marketplace. I am recovering the claim that Jesus Christ was not crucified on an altar between two candles, but on a cross between two thieves, on the top of a garbage heap, at a place so cosmopolitan that they had to write his name in Hebrew, Latin, and Greek, at a place where cynics talked smut, thieves cursed, and soldiers gambled.
>
> But that is where he died, and that is what he died about, and that is where Christians must be.
> —G. McLeod

world, even as I am not of it. Sanctify them by the truth; your word is truth" (John 17:14-17).

Second, the church must focus on the ministry of consolation and mercy. With fear becoming all-pervasive, people will hope to find in their church a haven of safety and protection. Overcome by loneliness, they expect to find in their church a form of genuine fellowship.

How can you as an elder contribute toward a ministry equipped to meet such awesome challenges?

1. Never underestimate the power of prayer. Great revivals in history were always the result of believers joining in prayer. And those revivals often were God's means of transforming societies and restoring a measure of well-being to the nations.

2. Officebearers must see to it that the local church's ministry has a dual focus: the well-being of its members as well as outreach to the world. Where that is the case, evangelism, the practice of mercy, and the kingdom pursuit of justice will be prime concerns.

3. Our churches everywhere are discovering the blessings of being involved in a variety of projects aimed at alleviating suffering, poverty, and distress. We often read of young people going to depressed areas at home and abroad, repairing homes, and building schools, churches, and medical clinics. Christian Reformed people use their political influence to advance causes of justice and mercy in Canada and the United States. Members come together to discuss how they can best sound a Christian testimony in their workplace. As an elder, be sure to support such important initiatives.

Remember to keep the vision alive: in the world, not of the world, and yes, *for the world.*[1]

Note

1. See *Our World Belongs to God,* sec. 17-18; and *Motivating Members for Ministry.*

MAKING A FAMILY VISIT

There was a time when most consistories visited the homes of most members of the church once a year. Such "home visits" may have seemed more like meddling than ministry, but generally the practice of home visitation has been a source of blessing in our churches. Many churches still retain this time-honored institution, and they are the richer for it. The tradition is a good one with ancient roots: Paul visited believers from house to house (Acts 29:20).

Article 65 of the Church Order stipulates that an "annual home visitation" be made. Why conduct an "annual home visitation"? Basically the purpose is to encourage, strengthen, and affirm family members in their personal faith (Eph. 3:14-21; 4:11-16).

You can do that by centering the discussion on such matters as an individual's relationship to the Lord, the certainty of salvation, the ground of certainty, the expression of faith in daily life, habits of the faith, relationships of Christian love, and so on.

You come as a representative of your Sender, Christ himself. So lay aside all trepidation and fear. You do not lean on much learning or on your "people skills"; you come armed with the gospel and a sincere desire to help family members be more firmly grounded in their faith.

How to do it

Following are some helps on how to call on a family with both parent(s) and children present. (We will devote separate chapters to visiting single members, the sick, those with burdens, the aged, and the bereaved.)

1. Schedule the visit well ahead of time. As a rule of thumb, schedule two visits per evening. Review your logbook entries regarding this family.

2. Before you ring the doorbell, say a prayer for this family and for yourself and ask for God's blessing on the visit. Pause a moment and assess yourself: Is your mind crowded with pressing personal concerns? Do you feel relaxed? Do you feel positive about this visit? Place these concerns into God's hands so they won't affect the visit.

3. As you are seated, remind yourself to pay attention to the family members. Observe the setting of the visit: furniture, pictures, newspapers, magazines, books. Perhaps they tell a story. What do they say about this family's interests?

4. Show your appreciation to your hosts for receiving you. Inquire about their well-being. Don't hesitate to ask some follow-up questions. Be sure to engage the

children at this time too. Open your time together with prayer.

5. As you inquire about the family's well-being, listen to what they tell you about themselves, then connect it to God's care and provision: Have they thanked him for the positive things they have reported? Have they prayed about hardships they have mentioned? You can then add a word of explanation and encouragement. You may also read a Bible passage that you have selected especially for this visit. See the box starting in the next column for suitable passages. Then ask questions about the passages and add some words of application.

6. The hub of the visit is a discussion of the family's walk with the Lord. You may want to raise some of the following questions:

> How are the members of this family assured of salvation?
>
> How have they experienced the forgiveness of sin?
>
> Can they discuss their religious experiences together?
>
> What pattern do they use in reading the Bible?
>
> In what ways are they blessed in their prayer life?
>
> What is their relationship to Christ as the foundation of their redemption?
>
> In what specific ways do they serve the Savior?

7. Be a sensitive listener. Try to understand the family's basic concerns. What seems to matter most to them? Do they indirectly refer to problems that are diffi-

---

Suggested Readings for Pastoral Visits

Saved by grace
Romans 5:5-11
Romans 7:14-25
Romans 8:1-8
Ephesians 1:3-10
Ephesians 2:1-10

Forgiveness and blessings
Psalm 32:1-7
Psalm 51:1-13
Psalm 130
Isaiah 40:1-8
Isaiah 53:1-9
Luke 15:11-24

God helps his people
Psalm 46
Psalm 91:1-8
Psalm 108
Psalm 121
Psalm 145:8-21
Isaiah 40:9-17
Isaiah 40:21-26
Matthew 6:25-34
Matthew 7:7-14
Luke 12:22-31
Ephesians 3:14-21

Invitation to godly living
Isaiah 55:1-9
Luke 14:1-14
John 3:11-15
John 15:1-17
Romans 12:1-8
Romans 12:9-21
2 Corinthians 9:6-15
Ephesians 6:10-20
Philippians 2:12-18
Colossians 3:1-17

God's good promise
Psalm 34:1-10
Psalm 62:5-8
Psalm 63:1-8
Luke 11:5-13
John 14:15-21

Joy of Christian living
Ephesians 3:14-20
Matthew 5:1-11
John 15:1-17
1 Corinthians 13
Philippians 1:3-11
Philippians 4:2-9
Colossians 1:9-14
2 Peter 1:3-11
1 John 4:7-20

Assurance in hardships
Psalm 23
Psalm 71:19-24
Psalm 77:1-15
Psalm 116
Psalm 124
Psalm 138
Romans 8:18-27
Romans 8:28-39
2 Corinthians 4:1-12

Praise
Psalm 33:1-11
Psalm 33:12-22
Psalm 47
Psalm 67
Psalm 93
Psalm 96
Psalm 97
Psalm 98
Psalm 99

Psalm 100
Psalm 103:1-8
Psalm 146
Psalm 147:1-11

Delight in God's will
Psalm 1
Psalm 19:7-14
Romans 8:12-17
Romans 12:9-21

Christian unity
John 17:20-26
1 Corinthians 1:10-17
1 Corinthians 3:1-15
1 Corinthians 12:12-31
Ephesians 4:1-13

Healing in sickness
2 Kings 5:1-15
John 4:46-54
John 5:1-19

Comfort in sorrow
Psalm 23
Isaiah 43:1-5
Isaiah 49:8-13
Isaiah 61:1-3
John 14:1-7
Romans 8:18-39
1 Corinthians 15:20-28
1 Corinthians 15:50-58
2 Corinthians 1:1-11
1 Thessalonians 4:13-18
2 Thessalonians 2:13-17
Hebrews 4:14-16
Revelation 7:9-17
Revelation 21:1-4

cult for them to bring out into the open? Don't hesitate to probe gently, but respect their right to privacy. Don't push if they are not ready to reveal details. Assure them that if they would like to discuss a certain matter in more detail later, you will be happy to make a follow-up call.

8. Be sure to guide the discussion. Don't let it stray from the purpose of your visit. Keep your focus on the relationship of this family to the Lord and how that works out in their daily lives.

9. Don't overstay your welcome. The visit should last about an hour. If you cut off small talk appropriately and ask questions connected with your mission, a lot of ground can be covered in one hour. Again, when difficult problems surface, schedule a follow-up visit.

10. If you did not read an appropriate Bible passage at the beginning of your visit, be sure to do so at the conclusion. Before the home visit season begins, make a list of suitable passages. Try to select one from your list that is in keeping with the discussion of the evening.

11. A closing prayer is appreciated by most families. The prayer should be marked by a loving concern for the family and include items of praise and intercession gleaned from your visit.

12. Should children participate in the visit? Yes. You may wish to suggest that they be present when you schedule the visit with their parents. It is very edifying to children to hear their parents' personal testimony. Tactfully draw the children

Joel had just been elected an elder and was about to make his first family visit. He approached that event with some fear. Fortunately he was teamed up with an older elder who had served several terms.

Joel said to his teammate, "To be honest, I find it very hard to talk about spiritual things. I am not looking forward to this visit." His older colleague said, "I know what you mean, but remember God is part of everyday life."

As the visit began, the older elder asked the father about his work. The father answered that his company had been laying people off and that he was not sure whether his job was secure. The older elder spoke words of empathy and understanding. He then asked the father if he had been able to pray about these painful realities, and whether he had been able to put his trust in the Lord now that the future was so uncertain. He also asked the mother of the family if she had found it possible to encourage her husband and whether she had been able to place her trust in her God.

Joel listened to this conversation with deep respect. He realized that these parents and the older elder were discussing their relationship to the Lord in a way that was totally genuine and devoid of artificiality.

into the discussion. Ask them about their lives and about their faith. Assure them of the Lord's covenant faithfulness.[1]

Here are a few things to avoid:

- Don't argue. In case of disagreement, express your conviction or speak a word of Christian testimony without becoming defensive.
- Don't talk much about yourself.
- Avoid trivia. Some small talk may help break the ice, but keep it to a minimum.
- Don't get stuck on one topic. If you run into a big problem, schedule a follow-up visit.
- Don't attempt to fill every moment of silence after you have spoken, even if the silences make you uncomfortable. You show people respect by giving them time to respond.
- Avoid "closed-ended" questions that can be answered by "yes" or "no."
- As a rule of thumb, don't solicit criticism of church practices, policies, or the pastor. Your visit focuses on the relationship of this family to God. Assure your people that the council is always willing to receive their suggestions and questions regarding the church's ministry program and practices. Should the misgivings clearly indicate deeper problems, make a follow-up call.
- Don't get bogged down in a discussion of issues. Again, there are better forums for members and officebearers to dialogue about issues.
- Don't shy away from discussing disagreeable subjects as long as they are germane to the family's walk with the Lord. Be aware, however, of your own limitations. If the faith-problems appear to be too complex, seek the help of others with special competence.

- Don't be a problem solver. Your people have the right to carry their own problems. You have come to affirm them in the Lord and assure them of his nearness.

Reporting to the consistory

Your visit was basically confidential. The members spoke from the heart. What they said should remain between them and you, their elder.

Should the members alert you to a trend in congregational life or express a concern about some church matter, ask if they want you to report their concern to the council or consistory. If they agree, be sure to inform them at a later date of the council's response. (See also section 41.)

When a visit turns out well, you may report your positive evaluation to the consistory as a matter of thanksgiving. When a visit turns out badly, you may express your concern to the consistory, without mentioning details, as a matter for intercessory prayer.

After a season of home visits and appropriate feedback, elders are in a better position to assess the spiritual health of the congregation and to devise a program of effective pastoral care.

Note
1. For helpful material see *Guiding the Faith Journey,* pp. 21-24, 59-63, 101-107.

VISITING SINGLE MEMBERS

As many as half of the people in your district may be single, divorced, or widowed. Your mission in visiting these members is basically the same as in visits to traditional families. The observations and suggestions in the previous section hold true for single members.

But keep the following in mind:

1. A single person may be intimidated by having two visitors. Be as disarming as you can be.

2. Never go alone to visit a single member of the opposite sex. This does not preclude, of course, the necessary ministry of visiting elderly shut-ins who may be of the opposite sex.

3. Single people may feel more comfortable visiting with you in a restaurant or other public place. You may feel that way too. If you agree to do so, make arrangements accordingly.

4. Single people may deal with life situations and challenges that are unfamiliar to you. Be a careful listener and a quick and sympathetic learner.

5. Sometimes a single member will not want to visit with you at all. He or she may, instead, prefer another form of personal interaction, such as a group meeting or a prayer circle. In fact, the trend among members in general seems to be to seek pastoral affirmation in such settings rather than through the traditional home visit. Personally, I hope that home visiting continues in the churches, but I

> There will be an increase of single parents in the churches. They face the heartless demands of life for which their material and mental resources are never a match.

also acknowledge that pastoral care can be provided in a variety of settings. As a district elder, make sure you attend such group meetings occasionally in order to maintain contact with members who attend.

6. Are single members lonelier than married people? Not necessarily, but be mindful of that possibility. Be ready to express your sympathetic concern if you sense the need. However, remember that your single member may not be lonely at all. He or she may have a great variety of satisfying friendships. Rejoice with single members who have such relationships.

7. Your church body should be careful not to make single members feel like second-class members by unguarded

remarks. Some think that the early Christian church stressed celibacy to the detriment of marriage. Today's church perhaps has gone too far in rehabilitating the married state. With that in mind, churches should orient ministry as much to individuals as to families.[1]

Single parents

Of special concern to you will be the single parents in your district. Life under normal circumstances is hard enough. Single parents face a whole set of problems and burdens beyond that. They miss the counsel and consolation husbands and wives give to each other. They often struggle with feelings of regret, anger, and rejection. Their income is probably very limited. They face all the demands of raising children alone. Meaningful friendships are hard to establish. Logistical problems are harder to solve. The work is never done. Moments of rest and reflection are rare.

Despite your busy schedule as an elder, don't scrimp on ministering to single parents. Their needs are many and must not be overlooked. Enlist the pastoral and material help of the deacons as you minister to this most important segment of your church body.

Note
1. See also *Our World Belongs to God*, sec. 48. For Bible readings see the previous section.

MAKING A SICK CALL

Illness is troubling for most people. Not only does it bring discomfort and pain, but it creates secondary problems in such areas as personal faith, family, marriage, work, economic well-being, and so on.

Sickness and pain are frequently mingled with vague feelings of guilt and failure. The sick often experience fear, and fear immobilizes. However, discussing their illness helps to relieve the fear and restores the sick to good confidence and courage. That's why James advised the sick to call in the elders (James 5:13-16). The form for Ordination of Elders and Deacons advises elders to "bear up God's people in their pain and weakness."

Here are some things to keep in mind in your ministry to the sick:

1. "Health" is related to the word "whole." Ill people experience lack of "wholeness" not only in the body but also in their inner being. They don't feel whole as persons. That's why your ministry to the sick should first be one of affirmation: this sick person is a full member of the church; he or she is whole in Christ; he or she has a worthy place in the community of believers.

2. Be informed. Don't pretend to be a medical authority, but remember what the patient chooses to entrust to you. Be discreet in asking details. Sick people will tell you what they want you to know.

3. Avoid giving the impression that you are in a hurry to leave, but don't overstay

I had considered hospital visiting as part of my professional life. I came to like those visits. I would see "my people," then make the rounds in the wards, spending a few moments at each bed. For me, time spent in hospitals was time well spent. That it had also become routine did not occur to me. . . .

Then one day our young daughter was hospitalized with a ruptured appendix. The doctors looked serious as she was wheeled into the operating room. The surgery took a long time. We waited and prayed and sat mostly in anxious silence. Later we sat at her bed where she lay with eyes closed as if concentrating on another world within her, cheeks fever-flushed. And we visited through a week of recuperation. Every visit came with new feelings of relief, love, and memories.

Hospital visits have not been quite the same since.

your welcome. People in pain prefer a short visit to a long one.

4. When the sickness is of somewhat longer duration, make regular visits. You may wish to keep contacts somewhat varied: visits may be interspersed with phone calls and cards. If a person doesn't hear from you for an extended time, you cannot hope to be of great significance in his or her life.

5. Remember that sickness affects a believer's faith life. A sick person ponders many questions: What is the purpose of this trial? What role does prayer play in my healing? Do I deserve this sickness? Are there spiritual reasons for my sickness? How does this affect people in my life? And, most importantly, how does God figure in my illness?

Don't attempt to answer these hard questions, but do sympathize in these struggles of the soul. Do more listening than talking. Avoid pat answers, but don't hesitate to assure the sick person that God is faithful, a hearer of prayer, and endless in his compassion and love. The following passages from the Psalms will provide comfort: 23:4; 27:1, 13-14; 62:1, 7-8; 71:1-3; 77:10-15; 91:1-6; 116:1-7; 118:28-29; 121:1-2, 7-8. (See also the list of Bible passages in section 19.)

6. Chronically ill people need your help to keep in touch with the life of the Christian community. Explore ways to ensure open lines of communication. Ask if the patient would like you to arrange for others to visit regularly.

7. When two people visit, it is natural that they tell about themselves. As a visiting elder, however, keep talk about yourself to a minimum. In general, avoid talking about illnesses you may have had or the illness of others.

8. Keep your closing prayer brief. Center on the well-being of the patient without spelling out medical details. Pray for healing when appropriate, for strength, courage, endurance, and the nearness of God. It is also proper to invite the patient to express a prayer request.

MINISTRY TO THE ELDERLY

They worked hard, they did much for the church, they developed many skills, but now they feel superfluous, unneeded, and, many times, lonely. They are the elderly in your congregation. Their number is growing. In many churches, 20-40 percent of the members soon will be counted among the elderly.

As you minister to elderly members, keep these things in mind:

1. The elderly appreciate regular, brief visits. One consistory devised a simple monthly plan to visit the elderly and shut-ins according to a four-month cycle which is regularly repeated:

- Month 1: a visit from an elder
- Month 2: a visit from the pastor
- Month 3: a visit from a member of the congregational visiting team
- Month 4: a visit from a deacon

2. Elderly members struggle with faith problems as often as younger members of the congregation. They may feel insecure in their redemption. Some may feel attacked by powers of darkness. You are to "encourage the aged to persevere in God's promises," according to the ordination form. Tactfully invite elderly members to share these spiritual concerns with you.

3. Involve elderly members in church life. Look for ways in which these experienced people may serve. See to it that all printed church releases reach their mailboxes. Be sure to seek the advice of the elderly on congregational issues.

4. Remember that your elderly members have much life experience. They have heard and pondered many sermons and may very well be equipped to provide care for each other. It may take an encouraging word from you to give them the freedom to minister in this way.

Church leaders should be careful not to patronize the elderly, but rather to respect and esteem them. The elderly also need understanding: they face a world from which many of their contemporaries have been removed, a world that is constantly changing. It is a myth that old people cannot or will not change. They desire to be worthy participants in the processes that cause change.[1]

Note
1. Christian Reformed Home Missions has produced a helpful study entitled "Report of the Committee on Senior Ministries" (*Acts of Synod 1985*, p. 702).

MINISTRY TO YOUTH

The spiritual health of the children and teens in your church is of great importance. If the new generation is not a vital part of your congregation, your church life will suffer. Care for the young should be both pastoral (focusing on personal guidance) and programmatic (focusing on structured group activities). The ordination form urges you to "be a friend and Christlike example to children. Give clear and cheerful guidance to young people."[1]

A youth leader recently remarked that a critical issue for young people is interaction between the Christian family and secular society. The Christian family bases its values, language, and ideas on the truths of the Word of God. It expects allegiance and loyalty from its members. Society, on the other hand, offers competing values and alluring rewards. Young people must come to terms with this dilemma: will they be defined by the family's expectations or by the world's enticement? Young people struggle to understand who they are. They wonder about issues of sexual awareness and experience. They search for a framework of values in which they can find peace and security.

The great challenge for the church, then, is to assist in the spiritual formation of its youth by providing an effective teaching program, promoting fellowship and friendships, and adopting challenging service programs. What can you do as an elder?

1. In your consistory and council meetings, emphasize the importance of ministry to the young. Encourage your pastor to take a deep personal interest in the children and young people of the church. Consider whether your commitment to children and teens is adequately reflected in your church budget.

2. Show interest in the church's youth programs. Talk to the youth leaders now and then. Attend youth-oriented events occasionally. Stop by at young people's meetings for a few moments and speak a word of encouragement. Don't leave these gestures of interest only to the youth elder.

3. Become acquainted with the children and teens of your district. Know their names and keep records of events that are important to them. Maintain a comfortable level of contact with them. Be available for them. Once a trust relationship develops, they will feel free to talk about spiritual things with you. And in later life they will remember you as a source of blessing. Can you think of a richer legacy?

4. Church Order article 63 stipulates that prayer for children and youth is an obligation of every church.

5. Many of your young people are willing and capable workers. By all means incorporate them in the ministry of the church. You will find that the church leaders do more than minister *to* young people; they minister *with* young people. Many churches have a youth elder and/or a youth director on staff. Such leaders should remain close to the young people, but they should not take over from them. The focus of the work of elders and staff should be on spiritual guidance, encouragement, and empowerment.[2]

Notes

1. See Church Order article 63 for a clear statement regarding the importance of ministry to youth.

2. See *Guiding the Faith Journey,* pp. 105-107. Also see Wayne E. Oates, *A Practical Handbook for Ministry* (Louisville: Westminster/John Knox Press, 1992), pp. 170-180. For additional advice and ministry materials contact United Calvinist Youth, 1333 Alger SE, PO Box 7259, Grand Rapids, MI 49510 or PO Box 1100, Norwich, ON N0J 1P0. For Bible readings see section 19.

MINISTRY TO THE DISABLED

A very painful reality facing people with disabilities is that other members often do not treat them as equals. As an elder you must do all you can to prevent such prejudices. Here are some suggestions:

1. As soon as you are installed, seek out any members with disabilities in your district. Ask them about their disability. What are the implications for their life? Do they suffer from pain, discomfort, severe limitations, or loneliness? Try to

> Some years ago I injured my leg while on vacation. We had planned to visit Disneyland and, rather than canceling the outing, my wife offered to push me around in a wheelchair provided by Disneyland for people with disabilities. Things worked out fine, but we made one painful discovery. Whenever we entered a pavilion the officials would address instructions to my wife. They never looked at me in the wheelchair. Soon I lost all initiative. Whatever the officials and my wife decided, literally over my head, was fine with me.

sympathetically understand their limitations. People with disabilities do not seek pity. Rather, they simply appreciate the same thoughtful pastoral care you give to others with burdens (see *Acts of Synod 1992*, p. 622).

2. Explore with members with disabilities whether they are as active and involved in church life as they would like to be. Many people with disabilities are not challenged sufficiently to be full participants in the church's ministry. Try to assess whether they have gifts and skills that go unused.

3. Is your church facility barrier-free? If it is only partially accessible, have provisions been made for persons with disabilities to attend all functions? Are special hearing aids available for those with hearing loss? Is transportation available for people with physical disabilities? Do you offer programs for those with mental impairments?[1]

Note

1. The Friendship Series curriculum provides religious instruction for persons with mental impairments and helps prepare them for meaningful participation in church life. For more information, call toll-free 1-800-333-8300 or write Friendship, 2850 Kalamazoo Ave. SE, Grand Rapids, MI 49560.

For additional consultation and resource materials, contact the CRC Committee for Disability Concerns, 2850 Kalamazoo Ave. SE, Grand Rapids, MI 49560, or PO Box 5070, STN LCD1, Burlington, ON L7R 3Y8.

MINISTRY TO THOSE WHO SUFFERED ABUSE

Sadly, abuse takes place in Christian circles. Instances of abuse represent some of the most difficult pastoral situations.

Abuse comes in various forms. *Physical abuse* is any nonaccidental injury inflicted on another person. It is often a chronic pattern of behavior. In some cases, severe punishment is a form of abuse. *Sexual abuse* is the exploitation of a person, regardless of age or circumstance, for the sexual gratification of another. Sexual abuse includes either nonphysical contact, for example, photographing a nude child in graphic poses; or physical contact, for example, fondling the person's breast, crotch, or buttocks. *Emotional abuse* is using threats or manipulation to control another, to diminish another's self-esteem, or to demand dependency of another person. Emotional abuse can also be a chronic pattern of behavior and generally continues over a much longer period of time. All these forms of abuse do great emotional and spiritual harm long after the physical scars are healed and even in the absence of any physical damage.

In abuse situations, the abuser holds power over the abused. This power may be physical (due to age, size, or strength); it can also be emotional, for example, threatening to starve a child or destroying a child's toys. The abuser can also hold spiritual power over the victim—in cases where the abuser misuses a spiritual position or spiritual authority to control, exploit, or coerce someone. When people misuse legitimate forms of power and authority, the result is a betrayal of trust. Such betrayal by Christians to each other or by church leaders leaves deep spiritual wounds in the victim and offender.

The word "abuse" is most commonly used when the victim is a minor, an elderly person, or a person with a disability, regardless of age. In adult relationships, the forms of abuse described above are sometimes called domestic violence (if it occurs in the home) or harassment (if it occurs in the workplace). The concept of abuse is referred to in ecclesiastical settings as misconduct, inappropriate behavior, or ungodly conduct (see *The Manual of Church Government*, art. 83).

The Calvin College Social Research Center conducted a survey of abuse for the synodical study committee on abuse in 1989. The results of that survey indicate that 12 percent of adults in the Christian Reformed Church are identified as victims of physical abuse and/or neglect. In the same survey, 13 percent of CRC adults are identified as victims of sexual abuse, and 19 percent are identified as victims of emotional abuse. A stunning 15 percent identified themselves as perpetrators of abuse.

There seems to be no escaping the harsh reality that both victims and perpetrators of physical, sexual, and emotional abuse are worshiping in Christian Reformed churches each Sunday.

What is your role as an elder in abuse situations?

1. Believe the victim's story until the facts prove otherwise. Abuse thrives in secrecy. Indeed, rarely are there eyewitnesses who can testify as to the events that allegedly took place. The victim is often threatened, bribed, or coerced into keeping the secret—sometimes for many years after the events occurred. When a victim discloses a story of abuse to an elder, believing the story can be the first step in restoring the trust that was betrayed.

2. Do not conduct an investigation of the matter. The role of the elder is to provide support, comfort, advocacy, and to seek justice and reconciliation whenever possible. Those who have tried to investigate such matters usually have found themselves at odds with the victim, the offender, or both. Such investigations should be encouraged, but ought to be conducted by professionals from the community.

3. Elders can be resource persons for either victim or offender. They should become knowledgeable about books, videos, or articles on abuse, and should be familiar with counselors or therapists in the community to whom they can make referrals. Elders should quickly avail themselves of denominational personnel who are experts in the matter for advice and consultation.

4. Model appropriate, healthy relationships with victims and offenders. With victims, it is important to set good guidelines for meeting with each other so that they feel safe with you. Be respectful of intimacy issues and do not request details of the abuse. Refrain from asking for hugs or touches that might confuse the victim as to your intentions. With offenders, avoid helping them figure out why the abuse happened. Often offenders are afraid to examine their behavior and expose the shame that lies within them. Instead, do help to keep the offender accountable. While assuring offenders of your concern for their well-being, encourage them to take responsibility for their behavior and avoid blaming the victim or others. If necessary, you may be called upon to help enforce consequences.

5. Use ecclesiastical resources and structures. *The Manual of Church Government* gives direction for responding to allegations of and confessions of misconduct or ungodly conduct (see art. 78-84). Elders, along with deacons, are given authority to adjudicate such complaints. It is your duty to know and understand these processes when called upon to exercise them.

In addition to the Church Order, Synod 1997 approved two sets of guidelines to follow when allegations of abuse are made against a church leader. The guidelines are divided by the age of the alleged victim. The guidelines for responding to allegations by a minor emphasize the importance of working with local police and child protection authorities. In many communities, reporting allegations of abuse is the law, and you are required to abide by it.

The guidelines for responding to allegations by an adult recommend an independent advisory panel to review the allegations, to meet with the accuser and the accused and any witnesses either one may have to substantiate their claim, and to provide a summary to the elders. In this scenario, the elder needs to set aside his or her personal opinions about either alleged victim or alleged offender, and instead respond only to the evidence collected by this trained, advisory panel. (For more information about the guidelines for responding to allegations of abuse against a church leader, consult the *Acts of Synod 1997*, pp. 674-685).

Some pastoral considerations:

Abuse cases are highly emotional and tend to become quite complicated and chaotic. For those reasons, they become very difficult for elders and pastors. Victims and their families express feelings of anger, confusion, fear, distrust, and shame. Offenders and their families may express some of the same feelings in addition to strong feelings of denial and indignation. All parties are concerned about their reputation and especially the perceptions of the church community to the allegations and to themselves. That is why the assistance and advice of Christian professionals and denominational personnel trained in this area are necessary in abuse matters.

Elders should not shy away from facing these difficult situations. It will serve them well to increase their awareness of the dynamics of abuse and to avail themselves of training and education about the issue. Abuse is rarely an isolated occurrence; more often it is a long-standing pattern. If an elder or pastor cannot face the trauma of the disclosure of abuse or respond effectively to the alleged offender, it seems inevitable that there will be other victims. Somewhere in the future the matter will arise again with no less heartache than the first time.

In addition, individual churches should have a child abuse prevention policy for use in case of allegations of abuse by a minor. A set of policies and procedures for responding to allegations by an adult victim would also serve the church well. An abuse response committee in each church could serve as a community resource link, an educational resource, a reporting committee, and as a group trained to respond effectively to either victim or offender. You may also consult with and obtain resource materials from the Office of Abuse Prevention, 2850 Kalamazoo Ave. SE, Grand Rapids, MI 49560.

Helpful resources on abuse include *Too Close for Comfort: Understanding and Responding to the Reality of Abuse* (Grand Rapids, Mich.: CRC Publications, 1994) and *Preventing Child Abuse: A Guide for Churches* (Grand Rapids, Mich.: CRC Publications, 1997), both by Beth A. Swagman. See also *A Survey of Abuse in the CRC* by Rodger R. Rice and Ann W. Annis (Grand Rapids, Mich.: Calvin College Social Research Center, November 1991).

26

MINISTRY TO THE HOMOSEXUAL MEMBER

In 1973 Synod approved a study on the nature of homosexuality and also made numerous suggestions for pastoral care to the homosexual neighbor *(Acts of Synod 1973,* pp. 50-53; 609-633). Synod said that "homosexuality" denotes a condition of personal identity in which one is sexually oriented toward persons of the same sex. Synod went on to declare that "homosexualism" refers to explicit homosexual practice.

The approved report states that "homosexuality is a condition of disordered sexuality . . . for which the homosexual may himself bear only minimal responsibility . . . and he may not be denied community acceptance. . . . If he is a Christian he is to be wholeheartedly received by the church as a person for whom Christ died."

Synod said that "homosexualism as explicit homosexual practice must be condemned as incompatible with obedience to the will of God as revealed in Holy Scripture" *(Acts of Synod 1973,* pp. 51-52).

Synod's pastoral advice includes the following guidelines:

1. Ministry to the homosexual neighbor should be marked by priestly compassion and concern. "The gospel of God's grace in Christ is to be proclaimed to him as the basis of his forgiveness, the power of his renewal, and the source of his strength to lead a sanctified life."

2. Synod called homosexuality a disorder and urged the churches to help homosexual members do everything within their power to overcome the condition, especially in their earlier years. Christian acceptance and support of these members can be a big factor in helping them to seek therapeutic aid. Many young members may have avoided seeking help from fear of detection and subsequent ostracism. Those who are not healed must accept the limitations of their homosexuality, and the church must minister to them as it would to all who are not married.

3. Acceptance is a big factor. Heterosexuals experience the same power of sexual temptation as do homosexuals. As confessing believers, all deserve the opportunity to serve the Master in various capacities and with equal honor in congregational life.

4. Pastors and district elders have a special challenge to minister to homosexual members, understand their plight, and also to minister, when appropriate, to such members' parents. They should also

do what is necessary to dispel prejudice from the ranks of the congregation.

5. Can homosexual members serve as officebearers? Yes, synod said. "Churches should recognize that their homosexual members are fellow-servants of Christ who are to be given opportunity to render within the office and structures of the congregation the same service that is expected from heterosexuals" (Acts of Synod 1973, p. 52).

6. It is now known that psychological aberrations in family and married life can contribute toward the sexual inversion of children. Churches should do all they can to promote healthy family relations. When parents observe disorders in their children's sexual maturation, they should not hesitate to seek Christian counsel (Acts of Synod 1973, pp. 50-53).

27

MINISTRY TO THOSE WITH MARRIAGE PROBLEMS

Can you minister effectively to couples struggling with marriage problems? Yes, you can. Remember, however, that you are not a marriage counselor. You may be equipped to discuss common marriage problems, and you may even give some helpful advice, but when it becomes clear that the couple faces a serious rift, then, by all means, suggest that they seek the help of a competent, Christian marriage therapist.

Does referral to a Christian counselor necessarily conclude your ministry to the couple? No. You continue what you were called to do as an elder: minister to the couple in the name of Christ.

What can the elder do?

1. Stay close to the couple with marriage problems. They tend to avoid contacts with others and will often experience a sense of isolation and loneliness. Your expression of concern will address a deeply felt need.

2. Assure the couple that God loves them. Where husband and wife feel isolated from each other, they may well feel isolated from God. God's love is unconditional. The couple may not have foreseen the trouble that has entered their marriage. Now they feel unworthy, betrayed, bewildered, and afraid.

3. Remain impartial. Don't assign blame to either partner. Direct the partners to examine their own ways critically and to confess wrongs to each other and to God. Weaknesses and shortcomings, once considered and confessed, are forgiven and not held against the other.

4. Try to teach the partners a constructive discussion pattern. Dialogues between husband and wife that are marked by an argumentative, accusatory, and reproachful tone do far more harm than good. Suggest that they agree to take turns in explaining dispassionately what really hurts them and what it would take to come to a better marriage arrangement and a restoration of love. Propose that they listen to each other without interruption. See if you can summarize some of the important things that each partner states.

5. Explore with the couple whether they will agree to establishing the following arrangement. With your help, both husband and wife select a mentor: a man for the husband, a woman for the wife. The two mentors should be selected for their spiritual maturity and personal wisdom. They should be secure people who are sympathetic and compassionate, but also firm and candid.

Husband and wife agree to establish honest relationships with their mentors and to consult with them in every significant step taken or decision made. From time to time you may arrange for a group meeting of the couple, the mentors, and yourself.

6. There will come a point, especially when progress is slow or cooperation minimal, when you have to ask either partner whether he or she is having an affair. Insist on hearing the truth. Don't hesitate to confront and to probe. If one admits that this is indeed so, you face a situation for which the previous points are inadequate. The pastor should now be brought in if that has not been done previously.

Healing is out of reach unless the affair is ended, sin is confessed earnestly, and professional help is sought seriously. Church discipline may be necessary if there is no repentance.

Should the couple wish to work hard at restoration with the help of marriage therapists, you will continue pastoral care. If divorce becomes a reality, you give as much care as the individual parties will welcome.

The dynamics of marriage problems are complex. If you try to follow the steps outlined above and you find that you are not equal to the challenge, do not hesitate to insist that the couple seek professional help. Your role would then be that of a friend and companion along a rocky road.

MINISTRY TO THOSE WITH ECONOMIC PROBLEMS

Economic life has become more unpredictable than ever. In some sectors fabulous profits are accumulated; in others good and able people are suddenly excluded from the economic cycle and left to exist on greatly reduced incomes. Some of these unfortunate people may sit next to you in church on Sunday. Their number may well increase in the coming years.

These people struggle with loss, fear, depression, and the pain of rejection. There is no single way to minister to them. The officebearers must become aware of such people and devise forms of ministry in keeping with their needs. Above all, don't hesitate to take the initiative in visiting them and asking how they are doing. In almost all cases, elders are not able to contribute significantly to solutions. Those who struggle with the pain of economic misfortune will not expect that from you.

Still, do explore some possibilities. Are there people in your congregation who specialize in financial management? If so, suggest that your members consult with them. You must also seek advice and possible assistance from the deacons. In more general terms, bring these economic challenges to the attention of the entire council. If one of your district members suffers financial hardship, the entire congregation hurts.

Continue also to minister to these members pastorally. They need to see you regularly. Encourage them, read Scripture with them, pray with them. Do whatever you can to keep these people from isolating themselves from the congregation.

MINISTRY TO THE BEREAVED

Ministering to the bereaved is a difficult task. After many years in ministry I still feel uncertain of myself in consoling the grieving. However, you can be a blessing to sorrowing people without being a trained grief counselor.

The following thoughts may help you:

1. The bereaved will initially go through a stage of numbness. They cannot immediately absorb the reality of their loss. That's why recently bereaved persons may appear to be strong and well-composed. It is not at all helpful to praise the grieving person for his or her apparent strength and courage. Once the numbness wears off, a relapse will occur. Be alert to the stages of grief. Before acceptance becomes a reality, the bereaved will experience deep feelings of denial, helplessness, anger, and despair.

The comfort provider should carefully avoid attempts to change the grieving pattern and to short-circuit the stages through which the bereaved person must go. For these reasons you would do well not to be solution-oriented in your ministry to those who are mourning. You bring a measure of support, but you cannot alleviate grief. Even well-intentioned attempts in that direction are uncalled for. The place made empty because of the death of a spouse or child or friend cannot be filled. Grieving is not to be equated with sickness from which people need to be healed. Life changes after bereavement; it is unalterably different. For fellow church members to expect the bereaved to "get over" their grief is inappropriate.

Literature on grieving points out that there are less-than-commendable ways to grieve. As with all human emotions and experiences, that is probably true. However, if you think it your duty to correct the grieving, you will probably make matters worse. Many grieving people come to a place of peace via painful detours. Many make "progress," then suffer setbacks. In the end they will be grateful that you were there for them.

2. Bereaved people need strength to cope with and to adjust to irretrievable loss. Can you, as their elder, help? Yes, to a modest degree you can. Be sure to make yourself available. Be present to listen and to offer fellowship. It is helpful for a sorrowing person to tell his or her story. By sharing the details of how it happened and how it hurts, the bereaved person gains strength, a little bit at a time. The process will take some time. Let it happen.

3. Be patient. Sorrow is a worthy component of your congregation's spiritual

and emotional mix. You need not, even at a subconscious level, be eager to have it removed from the congregational scene.) A congregation living with the reality of grief in its ranks will more readily depend on the Lord. (So continue your loving companionship with grieving members without being worried about "progress.") Those now grieving will be thankful for your assuring presence.

(4. Keep an eye on the calendar. Note the date of the loved one's death, and his or her birthday. Those are the days when the pain of grief hits hard. Send a signal to the bereaved that you understand.) Certain times of year, such as Christmas and Thanksgiving, accentuate the stark absence of the deceased. Note also that the second anniversary of the loss can be particularly hard for the survivors. They now realize fully that the irreversibility of death must be accepted. This is also the time when people assume that the bereaved are "over" their grief and should have returned to a "normal life." Stop by for a bit of reminiscing—it will be appreciated. As an elder never grow weary of praying for the bereaved.

We Jove You.
We Will Pray For You.
Touch
You were there.

Psalm 23
John 14
1st. Thes. 4 13-18

Prayer
Keep in touch!

Note

For additional help in dealing with grieving persons see Wayne E. Oates, *A Practical Handbook for Ministry* (Louisville: Westminster/John Knox Press, 1992), pp.137-140 and James R. Kok, *Waiting for Morning: Seeking God in Our Suffering* (Grand Rapids, Mich.: CRC Publications, 1997).

MINISTRY TO THE DYING

You will not sit at many death beds. Still, as an elder you must give prayerful attention to ministering to the dying and to the surviving loved ones.

1. Those who are terminally ill have a right to accurate medical information, including the physicians' diagnosis and prognosis. If medical evidence suggests that a patient will die, he or she should be informed, though you are not the person to do that. You may, however, with due discretion, advise the family members accordingly. They and the doctors should decide how to proceed.

2. Always be ready to listen carefully to what the dying person wants to tell you. When he or she expresses guilt or regret, don't respond with easy assurances. Such feelings are probably of long-standing and weigh heavily on the patient. Give ample time for the person to explain. Then, on behalf of Christ, your Sender, you may speak words of forgiveness free and complete through the Savior. God will not remember these sins any longer. The slate is clean, as far as God is concerned. If possible, invite the patient to accept that forgiveness, then pray for assurance and express thanks to God for so great a salvation.

3. Terminally ill people may express deep worry about the well-being of their loved ones. Such concerns should not be taken lightly. If possible, allow for some discussion and explanation. Then read some verses from the Bible that testify to God's care for his people, such as Psalm 23; Psalm 37:25; John 14:1-4; John 17:13-18; and Romans 8:1-8. God will never give up on his people. He will care for them. Always. Assure the dying of the reality of the unsurpassed bliss of eternal life. Use such passages as 1 Corinthians 15:20-28, 50-58; Revelation 7:9-17; and Revelation 21:1-4.

4. Minister also to the family members. Each will cope with the death of their loved one in his or her own way. If possible, have them tell you how they feel and where they stand with the Lord. Loved ones and immediate relatives of the deceased will deeply appreciate your follow-up visits.

MINISTRY TO THE SUICIDAL

People with suicidal tendencies will often send a signal of distress. The pattern of their life may show sudden changes. They may become very depressed. They may take the initiative to have a will drawn up. They may say such things as "I'm tired of trying."

If family members alert you to such realities, advise that they seek competent professional help. You may wish to consult with the pastor. People near someone contemplating suicide should not hesitate to ask, "Have you thought of taking your life?" When family members (or you) find that such a person avoids overtures of help, take the initiative to arrange professional intervention.

As an elder, don't postpone acting on whatever signals come your way. Suicide is on the increase, especially among the young. Seek every opportunity to assure these desperate people that God is a God of mercy, acceptance, forgiveness, help, solutions, and new possibilities.

Maintain regular contact with them. Try to discuss questions like these: What do you think of the future? Do you have hope for life? Do you have plans for next summer? Are you enjoying your hobbies? Are you concerned about the company you work for, your family, your church? Have you experienced God's grace in Christ? Consistently evasive answers or lack of interest in anything relating to the future may indicate deep problems.

THE IMPORTANCE OF FOLLOW-UP GESTURES

The importance of follow-up care cannot be overemphasized. You are a blessing to your people not only by what you say in your visits but also by who you are as a shepherd to them. That reality alone is a consolation to your people. You represent the Lord and his people. Your very office is an assurance to the members that they belong to the body of believers, the body of Christ.

That's why follow-up gestures are so important. Follow-up care validates your initial pastoral outreach. Your people feel affirmed and respected when you make a second contact. They conclude that your first visit meant as much to you as it did to them. You can make follow-up contact by another brief visit, by phone, or by sending a note.

The reverse may be true too: when your members don't hear from you after an initial visit, they may wonder how deeply you felt their burden. You will invariably find that follow-up gestures are appreciated out of proportion to the investment of time they require.

CHANCE ENCOUNTERS: MINISTRY OPPORTUNITIES

Of course, we understand that nothing happens "by chance." However, you will have ministry opportunities that are entirely unplanned. Don't underestimate the importance of these "chance" encounters.

Regularly checking your log or index system will keep you aware of your members and their circumstances. When you see them at congregational activities or spot one of them in the neighborhood shopping center, say hello. If you both have the time, take a few minutes to chat. Ask about the member's well-being. Add a word of encouragement. Make a mental note of important details and record them in your log later.

You may find that using such encounters constructively makes you a more outgoing and fulfilled person. And it means a lot to your people when they know you take the time to care. Ongoing contact is the very vehicle of your ministry.

Pay special attention to the children in your district. Know their names. Make them feel special by singling them out and paying attention to them. It is important for them to know that they too belong to the church.

Look on these chance encounters as divine appointments. They, indeed, occur according to God's divine will and should never be ignored or avoided.

BOUNDARIES

In your dealings with people, be sure to respect interpersonal boundaries.

You approach the members of your district as an officebearer. Keep it that way. Propriety and respect will then always characterize your contacts. Don't be overly formal, but avoid excess familiarity, which can lead to emotional dependence and romantic involvement. Draw firm boundaries around your person and your actions as an elder.

Also draw a boundary line around the power and prestige that you as an officebearer possess. Use them sparingly and only for the promotion of the kingdom. Also, consider the boundary between your personal life and your "life" as an officebearer. Don't be active in the one at the expense of the other. Seek a healthy balance.

The church has its own built-in boundaries without which it cannot function effectively. Church societies, committees, and leaders have their assigned responsibilities. As the consistory and council consider various initiatives, they must ask, "Which board, committee, or person will handle these tasks?" Don't overstep the boundaries of others' responsibilities.

Remember that you must keep in confidence everything told in confidence. I suggest that you go a step further: whatever you discuss with your members you keep to yourself. If people share information with you that you feel should be shared with others, seek permission first. See section 42 for further advice on discretion and confidentiality.

Elders, deacons, ministers, staff members, and church leaders may profit from the following guidelines.[1]

1. Be aware of the dynamics of sexuality in your relationships with parishioners and colleagues. Your pastoral position may invite peculiar temptations. Those whom you serve have their own needs and expectations. Deal with them respectfully and circumspectly.

2. Be honest about your own sexuality, your needs, and avenues of proper fulfillment so that at all times you conduct yourself in a morally proper way. Sexual dysfunction in your marriage poses a vulnerability in your pastoral work that must be resolved in cooperation with your spouse. Seek professional help when needed.

3. Safeguard healthy relationships in practical ways. If you are visiting a member of the opposite sex, take along your spouse. Visit early in the evening rather than late. A visit in a church facility with

people around is better than one in a deserted building. Doors with uncovered windows are better than solid ones. Doors ajar are better than doors closed.

4. Agree to be accountable to a colleague, spouse, or peer to ensure that you are maintaining proper boundaries and that you are clearly aware of where your feelings and fantasies are leading you.

5. Guard your spiritual, emotional, and physical well-being. Do your work with a positive, charitable attitude. Grudges and discontent will undercut your defense against temptation and self-destruction. Draw on the resources of faith and prayer to surmount discouragement, criticism, and loss of self-esteem—conditions that make you a ready target for the evil one.

Note

1. Adapted from *Acts of Synod 1994,* pp. 193-194.

4

PART 4

CONSISTORY AND COUNCIL

In Part Three we focused on the ministry of individual elders to members in their districts. In Part Four we will consider the organizational side of church life: how the elders, working together as consistory and council, assist the congregation's ministry in its various forms. Is the programmatic work of the elders less spiritual and less personal than the work they do individually among the members? Not at all. The goal is the same: to establish people in Christ. Church life functions best when sound organizational policies are in place.

Note again that "consistory" is the assembly of elders and minister(s). The "council" consists of the elders, minister(s), and deacons. On the following pages, when advice is given for the council, it also holds true for the consistory.

THE COUNCIL—A REMARKABLE INSTITUTION

Now that you have been ordained an elder, you belong to a remarkable institution: the church council. No other institution in society is quite like it. That is because the church itself and its government is unique.

The council is the regulatory body in your church, yet there is nothing absolute about its authority. The officebearers serve in subjection to Christ, the head of the church. They exercise their office not so much by governing as by supervising, or, better still, by serving. They follow the example of Christ, who said of himself that he came to serve rather than to be served (Matt. 20:24-28; John 13:1-17).

The council recognizes that the church members are, indeed, officebearers. They assume the office of believer and share in the anointing of Christ individually and corporately (Ex. 19:6; Gal. 6:2; 1 Pet. 2:5-10; 4:10; Heidelberg Catechism, Lord's Day 12). So the council will respect the mature judgment of the congregation and consult with the members on important issues. At the same time, the church is not a democracy. The council decides for the membership, being responsible to Jesus Christ, the head of the church.

Note also that though elders, deacons, and pastors may be ordained to different functions, they are equal "in dignity and honor" (Church Order, art. 2). In your council there is no place for a CEO. The officebearers make decisions collegially, and by consensus when possible.

The fundamental differences between the church and other institutions are summarized in article 1 of the Church Order:

> The Christian Reformed Church, confessing its complete subjection to the Word of God and the Reformed creeds as a true interpretation of this Word, acknowledging Christ as the only head of his church, and desiring to honor the apostolic injunction that in the churches all things are to be done decently and in order (1 Corinthians 14:40), regulates its ecclesiastical organization and activities in the following articles.

Your council works toward one goal: that the body of believers grows both in faith and in number. Some of that growth can be observed, perhaps even measured, but much of it only God can measure. The "product" of your work often remains invisible. You leave it to the Lord to determine how cost-effective your investment as an elder really is.

USING THE CHURCH ORDER

Your church is structured according to biblical standards. The council must see to it that the church remains true to the Word of God in its faith, practice, and organization. Your church, however, also faces many challenges that were unknown to the writers of the New Testament. The Bible does not address every specific situation we face today.

Many of the policies and practices of the Christian Reformed Church are guided by the Church Order of the Christian Reformed Church in North America. It is a venerable, time-tested document from which the denomination and its individual congregations have richly profited. Its roots lie in the church order drafted by the churches of the Reformation in Europe in the sixteenth century.

Our present Church Order reflects what we believe the Word of God mandates the church to be and to do. That is especially true of things essential to church government, but the Church Order also spells out provisions for the church that are circumstantial and situational. These provisions were made by common consent for which no immediate biblical grounds could be claimed. That's why through the years, as new needs and challenges arise, the Church Order is revised to serve the churches more effectively.

You will profit greatly from reading and consulting the Church Order regularly. It will deepen your appreciation for what the church of Christ is and how it can do its ministry best. Discord in church life often stems from a misunderstanding of procedural rules agreed upon by all.[1]

Note

1. *Church Order and Rules for Synodical Procedure* is updated annually. Copies may be ordered from CRC Publications, 2850 Kalamazoo Ave. SE, Grand Rapids, MI 49560. Call toll-free 1-800-333-8300 in the U.S. or Canada.

STRUCTURING THE COUNCIL

In the past, Christian Reformed councils functioned effectively with a simple structure. The minister served as president and chaired the monthly meeting; an elder was elected clerk and kept the minutes; a vice-president, or vice-all, took over when needed; and a treasurer took care of finances. The volume of business was such that a single monthly meeting was usually sufficient.

Through the years, however, as councils have had to deal with more diversified needs, they have refined their organizational arrangement. Now officers often meet separately as an executive committee. This group serves the full council (then still called "consistory") in a number of ways: by preparing the council agenda, by researching agenda items, and by performing routine council duties between meetings. Councils also appoint a variety of service committees to facilitate many congregational activities. The work of the deacons too has gained prominence, thereby relieving the council's workload.

Since the 1980s, councils have found that officebearers have less discretionary time than did their colleagues of a generation ago. The demands of leadership are steadily increasing. Many councils have divided their work into two broad areas: administering the overall support system for congregational ministries, and spiritual and pastoral caregiving. Such councils then assign the first area to the administrative council and the second to the pastoral council. Both councils meet monthly. The combined council meets perhaps no more than four times per church season, mostly for policy setting and review. The elders meet periodically as a consistory to deal with confidential pastoral matters. Though the Church Order has not specifically sanctioned this arrangement, it certainly does not contradict the spirit of the Church Order.

Some years ago, Synod reminded councils of their freedom to make stewardly arrangements in keeping with local needs and conditions:

"Because the Scriptures do not present a definitive, exhaustive description of the particular ministries of the church, and because these particular ministries as described in Scripture are functional in character, the Bible leaves room for the church to adapt or modify its particular ministries in order to carry out effectively its service to Christ and for Christ in all circumstances" (Acts of Synod 1973, p. 64).

As churches learn from each other, they will make further adjustments and corrections.[1] This will enable councils to assign responsibilities to gifted and skilled officebearers who, in turn, will be able to respond promptly to needs and opportunities. This development will surely benefit the church as changes are made in accord with biblical guidelines for church offices. (See section 50 for a discussion of the need for good communication within the church.)

Note
1. See also Dirk Hart, *New Designs for Ministry Structure* (Grand Rapids, Mich.: CRC Publications, 1996).

38

PREPARING THE COUNCIL AGENDA

The most common reason for unsuccessful council meetings is lack of preparation. In response, councils should designate a team of members to draft the agenda of the upcoming meeting. In most churches this task falls to the executive committee. A well-prepared agenda contributes greatly toward the success of the meeting.

The agenda should ensure continuity with previous meetings. The team should review the minutes of the previous two meetings and determine if any matters remain unresolved. It must then decide what needs to be done to facilitate action and may even suggest a possible solution for the council. (Keep in mind that ongoing "unfinished business" can drain the morale of officebearers.) Such planning will probably free some necessary time for such items as vision casting, dreaming, studying, planning, reviewing, and praying.

Officebearers should submit agenda items at least a week before the meeting so that the team has opportunity to consider whether each item belongs on the agenda. The team does not serve as the final arbiter of what the assembly will consider, but it may certainly assist in bringing matters to the assembly in the proper manner. (See also section 51.)

Here are some examples:

- Elder A. has a misgiving that he wants to air before the council. The team, however, advises that the elder first speak to the committee in charge of matters related to the elder's concern. To this advice Elder A. agrees.
- Deacon B. submits a proposal about which she feels deeply. The team advises her to first seek the input of her fellow deacons before putting the proposal on the agenda.
- Elder C. has a number of suggestions for improving the worship services. The team discusses with him the possibility of first consulting with the worship committee.
- Elder D. presents a proposal that the team recognizes as significant for the church's outreach program. The team agrees to place it on the agenda but secures Elder D.'s agreement that he first meet with the evangelism committee about it and see whether further research can be done. If need be, the council can take the matter up at a following meeting.
- Deacon E. wishes to place a question on the agenda. The team points out to him that council dealt with the matter the previous year and gives him a copy of the minutes. The deacon is satisfied but requests that mention be made of his concern. The team agrees

and places an informative item on the agenda.

- Elder F. requests permission for a service he wishes to perform. The team explains that for such a service no council permission is needed and encourages the elder to go ahead. They place the matter on the agenda as an informative item.
- Mr. G., a member of the congregation, proposes a change in the church's incorporation under the Society Act. The team places the matter on the agenda but asks Mr. G. to draft a background paper for the council's benefit. This he promises to do.

The team should distribute the agenda to the officebearers on the Sunday before the meeting date. The officebearers should be encouraged to study the agenda carefully prior to the meeting.

CORPORATE LOYALTY

As an elder you are both an individual with your own convictions and a member of a body of officebearers. That reality has important implications for your interactions with the members of your church.

1. You represent the council. You may have voted against a proposal that the body approved. Now you must support it and help to implement it. You should never speak against it to the members.

Article 29 of the Church Order stipulates that "decisions of the assemblies shall be considered settled and binding, unless it is proved that they conflict with the Word of God or the Church Order."

If you feel that a decision of your council is in conflict with the Word of God or the Church Order, you have the right of appeal to your classis, and, if necessary, to synod. If you choose that route, use utmost discretion in discussing your views with fellow church members.

2. Your council deserves a good reputation in your church. Without it, your council cannot provide effective leadership. Do your share in guarding and upholding that good reputation. Your council is not perfect. If you have criticisms, bring them to the council, not to the congregation.

3. Your council does not work in secrecy. The congregation is entitled to know what the council decides and why. Members are also entitled to the general substance of discussions, but not specifically to who said what, how it was said, whose names were mentioned, and other personal details. The council would do well to report its actions in the church bulletin, ensuring that confidentialities are guarded. Confidentiality should especially surround the pastoral work of the elders in the consistory meetings (*Acts of Synod 1991,* p. 723).

4. Corporate loyalty has wider implications. The members themselves should be loyal to the church and should uphold its good reputation. The council will remind the congregation of this sacred obligation whenever appropriate.

CONDUCTING THE ASSEMBLY MEETING

Which officebearer has not come home weary and deflated after a meeting that was long on discussion and short on accomplishment? Some of this is unavoidable, but consider these helpful suggestions:

1. The chair may remind the council members occasionally that the council is both a *deliberative* and a *decision-making* body. The discussion will remain on track when focused on the matter at hand. Decisions will be most helpful when carefully considered.

2. The chair should feel free to interrupt a free-wheeling discussion graciously and suggest that the discussion focus on the matter before the assembly.

3. When speakers repeat themselves or repeat what others have said, the chair should not hesitate to remind them gently that good arguments need not be stated often.

4. When the council is divided and it appears to feel deeply about the issue at hand, the chair may propose to postpone the matter until the next meeting. The chair may also appoint an advisory group to study the propsal and present their findings to the council at a later meeting.

5. Endless discussions often result from lack of good preparation. Officebearers intuitively sense whether a proposal has been carefully thought through, whether its ramifications have been understood, and whether its benefits are promising. Council leaders should insist that proposals be well researched before they reach the assembly.

6. When the council is divided on an important issue and a decision must be made in the same meeting, the chair should allow extra time for discussion. When no consensus emerges, the chair may suggest a brief recess, after which each officebearer is invited to make a summary statement. After that the vote is taken.

Councils are well served when decisions are made by consensus or with a substantial majority. Decisions made with a slim majority generally will not benefit the congregation. Councils would do well to agree to reconsider, at a subsequent meeting, matters passed by a narrow margin. Synod's procedural rules make it possible to reconsider and rescind matters decided in previous sessions.[1]

7. Long discussions and the inability to make decisions are often symptomatic of an assembly's inner division. The officebearers should honestly address such divisions. A series of informal meetings, preferably in a retreat setting, can be a

positive step when reflecting on the nature and task of the church and the needs of the local congregation. Outside advisers may be invited to provide guidance and counsel. (See section 60.)

8. Does your council use proper parliamentary rules of order? It is important to do so. The *Rules for Synodical Procedure,* though not applicable to council meetings in every respect, can be helpful.

9. The leaders of the council should be concerned about the interpersonal relationships of the officebearers. When relationships are strained or broken, meetings invariably become unproductive. The leaders should not hesitate to discuss with the parties concerned the need for reconciliation and offer their assistance in mediation efforts.[2] (See also section 48.)

Notes

1. *Church Order/Rules for Synodical Procedure* (Grand Rapids, Mich.: CRC Publications, 1997), p. 94. Available from CRC Publications, 2850 Kalamazoo Ave. SE, Grand Rapids, MI 49560 or call toll-free 1-800-333-8300. One updated copy is sent to each council after every synod.
2. For advice and resource materials contact the CRC General Secretary and/or the office of Pastor-Church Relations, both located at 2850 Kalamazoo Ave. SE, Grand Rapids, MI 49560. Call 616-241-1691.

41

ELECTING COUNCIL MEMBERS

Isn't it a small miracle that you are an elder? From the many names the council considered (and discussed!) yours was put on the slate of nominees submitted to the congregation. Another two weeks elapsed, during which time the congregation raised no objections against your nomination. Then you were elected. And then the council appointed you, and you were installed in the office of elder.

Now you are part of the process through which the council's ranks are replenished. Here are some important steps to include:

1. Involve the congregation from the start of the search process. Your council may solicit names from the congregation and also invite committees to suggest names. In fact, article 4b of the Church Order stipulates this.

2. A part of the nominating process is "discussing names" in the council meeting. The chair may remind the office-bearers that they must be honest and open, but that information regarding those considered for office must relate to their suitability for office only. None of the information should be accusatory. It should be clearly understood that the entire discussion remains strictly confidential.

3. What criteria do you use in nominating members to the office of elder? From 1 Timothy 3:1-7 and Titus 1:5-9 we learn that prospective candidates must be good and godly people, mature and reputable, wise and responsible. The candidates for this office should have stewardly gifts so they can "keep watch over . . . all the flock . . . [and] be shepherds of the church of God" (Acts 20:28). They must "desire" the office (1 Tim. 3:1). Though not every elder can be expected to be a gifted teacher, Scripture requires that elders be "able to teach" (1 Tim. 3:2).

4. At what point should the nominees be informed of their nomination? Some councils secure the permission of the prospective candidates before presenting their names to the congregation. The advantage is that, should certain candidates not be able or willing to serve, their names can be deleted before being publicly announced. The disadvantage is that some decline a bit too readily since they have not yet been nominated. For that reason other councils announce the full slate and place the onus on the nominees to decline with the entire congregation becoming aware of it. Such candidates are then under more pressure to provide good reasons for their unavailability. The trend seems to be to consult with candidates before making the final

list. That approach is also more sensitive to the dignity of the candidates.

5. "In calling and electing to an office, the council shall ordinarily present to the congregation a nomination of at least twice the number to be elected. When the council submits a nomination which totals less than twice the number to be elected, it shall give reasons for doing so" (Church Order, art. 4a).

6. Normally, a council will submit one list from which the congregation elects half (or more) of the names. However, in more recent years councils have felt the need to present "double nominations," or sets of two names from which the congregation selects one.

The council may, for instance, nominate two members with gifts for youth ministry and then place them as a duo on the ballot. Because some congregations may be spread out geographically, the council may draft duos of members living in specific districts. Council may also wish various age-groups to be represented and hence draw up duos of similar ages. Some spiritually mature members fail to be elected repeatedly. Councils then may put two such people on a duo. (See also *Acts of Synod 1983.*)

7. Synod opened the office of deacon to women in 1984 (*Acts of Synod 1984,* pp. 654-655). Synod of 1996 made provision for women serving as elders (*Acts of Synod 1996,* p. 550-551). Should your council wish to nominate women to the office of elder, it will need to first consult with the congregation. If women are

nominated, your council may wish to consider "double nominations" as described in the previous paragraph.

8. Note that the Church Order stipulates that election by the congregation shall take place at a regular congregational meeting under supervision of the council. Also, the right to vote is limited to confessing members in good standing. (See art. 4c; see also art. 37.)

9. In large congregations, or congregations that are quite spread out, it is important that council provide a profile of the candidates nominated for office and that they be introduced to the congregation.

10. Is it a good practice to select office-bearers by lot? Synod of 1985 did not favor the idea. Synod stated that "the use of the lot limits the responsibility of the office of the believer" and that "at the moment of choice [the member] is merely an observer" rather than a participant (*Acts of Synod 1985,* p. 714). Synod of 1989 confirmed that judgment (*Acts of Synod 1989,* p. 469).

Some churches use a combination of the regular election process and the casting of lots. The congregation elects twice as many names as are needed. The lot is then cast, selecting half of the candidates for appointment to their respective offices. Those who are not selected need then not feel rejected by the membership.

11. The names of those elected are ordinarily announced to the congregation on

the two Sundays prior to installation. Installation takes place in a worship service with the use of the appropriate form (Church Order, art. 4d). Synod adopted a form that distinguished between "ordination"—the ceremony in which any officebearer is brought into office for the first time, and "installation"—the ceremony in which the induction is for a subsequent term. (See *Acts of Synod 1983*, p. 643.)

12. How long should terms for elders be? Most elders serve a term of three years, usually with the understanding that they can be nominated again after a leave of one or two years. Some churches have two-year terms. That seems a bit short in view of the fact that it probably takes nearly a year for elders to get to know the members of their districts.

Article 25a of the Church Order allows for immediate eligibility for reelection if "circumstances and the profit of the church" make that advisable. "Elders and deacons who are thus reelected shall be reinstalled."

13. Article 4 does not mention laying on of hands as part of the ordination/installation ceremony. Synod, however, gave the churches the freedom to add this gesture as a symbol of the church having called the new officebearers to their particular tasks. "The ceremony of the laying on of hands is not a sacrament but a symbolic act by which the church may publicly confirm its call and appointment to particular ministries. As such it is useful but not essential" (*Acts of Synod 1973*, p. 64).

Synod stated that laying on of hands is appropriate for the ordination/installation of all four church offices, but added that the actual laying on of hands is to be performed by ministers and elders (*Acts of Synod* 1983, p. 643). Some churches have afforded deacons and evangelists the same privilege.

14. Some councils provide training for officebearers well before nomination time; others offer it to the newly appointed officebearers. In any case, training will bear much fruit.[1]

Note

1. For helpful material see *Acts of Synod 1973*, pp. 653-716. See also Remkes Kooistra, *Straight Talk—A Fresh Look at 1 Timothy* (Grand Rapids, Mich.: CRC Publications, 1996), pp. 49-55.

42

DISCRETION AND CONFIDENTIALITY

It has become second nature to you to be discreet. It now is a way of life for you never to discuss with third parties whatever your people have entrusted to you.

Councils should discourage officebearers from mentioning personal details of parishioners' lives in full meetings. This holds also for consistory meetings when elders report on home visits. Exceptions may be made when it is clearly for the parishioners' spiritual well-being. Even then a good check would be to ask yourself this question: How would this parishioner react if he or she heard me make these statements? In fact, a case could be made for parishioners having the right to know what officebearers report concerning them in assembly meetings.

From discretion to confidentiality is a small step. Confidentiality as a virtue in pastoral work is, of course, not new. The form for the Ordination of Elders and Deacons contains these phrases: "keeping in confidence those matters entrusted to them" and "hold in trust all sensitive matters confided to you."

What is new is that the matter of confidentiality is laden with judicial implications. In this litigious age people will not hesitate to sue when they feel betrayed

by someone in the helping professions (*Acts of Synod 1988,* p. 535).

Synod drafted important guidelines for councils. The report titled "Statutes, Rules, and Laws Related to Privileged Communication to the Clergy," containing statutory references as of 1987, is available from the office of the General Secretary (*Acts of Synod 1991,* pp. 723 and 769). Following is a summary:

1. Whatever parishioners tell you in confidence is privileged communication and is to be held inviolate by you.

There are two exceptions:

    a. if the confidential matter can bring serious harm to the one who told you or to others

    b. if the person who told you gives you permission to alert the proper authorities

Should a member share a difficult problem with you in confidence and you feel the need for competent advice, you may go to a specialist and lay out the problem "in the theoretical," safeguarding the identity of the member. You may also tell the member that you are unable to help and suggest strongly that he or she seek the aid of a specialist.

Bob and Joanne

Many things went wrong for Bob and Joanne when they lived in the western part of the country: employment problems, marriage tensions, and an unfortunate conflict in their local church. When they moved east, they saw it as a promising new beginning.

When Bob and Joanne's membership was transferred, the pastor enclosed a note for his colleague in the couple's new congregation, explaining some of the problems and commending them to his special pastoral care. The minister of the receiving church read the note to the elders. A week or so later, one of the elders made a welcome visit to Bob and Joanne. In the course of the conversation he told them that he was happy that they could have this new beginning. Bob, a straightforward man, asked the elder why he thought they needed a new beginning. The elder, equally straightforward, divulged the content of the previous minister's note.

Bob and Joanne felt hurt and disappointed. The visit ended in an impasse. A subsequent visit of the elder and the pastor with explanations and apologies brought some resolution, but the beginning in their new church was less happy than they had hoped.

Were communication mistakes made? How could they have been prevented?

2. The classical church visitors must make sure that local officebearers are aware of the need to protect confidential information.

3. Recognized church leaders have the right to refuse to testify in court as a matter of conscience regarding confidential information received in the performance of their duty.

4. Councils must be very circumspect in processing cases of church discipline. In making public announcements, the sin of the offending member should not be mentioned. State only that the member has not repented. Consistories would do well to seek legal counsel in complicated and protracted discipline procedures.

Synod also advised every church to state "its membership requirements very clearly, including the expectation that all members are to participate in and be subject to the admonition and discipline of the church" (*Acts of Synod 1991*, p. 723). Churches, in other words, must make it plain to their members that possible disciplinary steps are part of the conditions of membership.

43

THE CONGREGATIONAL MEETING

Councils cannot govern constructively unless they maintain close contact with the congregation. Wise councils regularly consult with the membership through congregational meetings. Thus, the congregation has a significant share in the overall administration of congregational life.

While article 37 of the Church Order stipulates that council shall "invite [the congregation's] judgment about . . . major matters" and that "full consideration shall be given to the judgment expressed by the congregation," it concludes by affirming that "the authority for making and carrying out final decisions remains with the council as the governing body of the church."

Christ is the head of the body of believers—the church. The officebearers rule in his authority, so they have the final responsibility for decisions made. They also recognize that the membership consists of mature believers who participate in the office of believer and whose judgment, therefore, is highly valued in the governing process.

Note that the Church Order recognizes three ecclesiastical "assemblies": council, classis, and synod. The congregational meeting is not one of those assemblies (art. 26). Rather the congregational meet-ing, technically, is a council meeting at which the congregation is invited to express its ideas.

A few more observations:

1. Congregational meetings must be held "at least annually" (art. 37), but wise councils will arrange for several a year.

2. Excluded from discussion in congregational meetings are matters "which pertain to the supervision and discipline of the congregation" (art. 37). Individual members can be sure that the personal ministry of the elders and pastors will never be divulged to other parties.

3. All professing members in good standing who are at least eighteen years old have voting privileges. That's why the meeting must be announced clearly, publicly, and well ahead of time.

4. Congregational meetings are conducted by the council. The president of council will normally chair the meeting and assume responsibility for conducting proceedings in an orderly and constructive way. (Note that Canadian law now insists that the whole membership must approve the budget. Technically, the members make the final decision, not the council.)

5. According to article 37, "only matters which (the council) presents shall be considered." This is an important point. A congregational meeting is called by council to consider matters that it has researched and with which it has struggled. Every member has the right to bring a matter before council for consideration. A member may even ask the council to address a certain matter in a congregational meeting. It is up to council, however, to decide whether it shall be placed on the agenda.

In some churches the meeting customarily concludes with the chair asking, "Does anyone have any further business?" In keeping with the spirit of article 37, such a question should be omitted.

Proposals adopted at a congregational meeting must be considered and adopted by the council before they are implemented. These actions should be communicated to the congregation.

In the rare instance that council is unwilling or unable to implement a proposal passed at a congregational meeting, it will arrange for another congregational meeting at which explanation is made and further advice sought. The council must also ascertain if its desires contradict the congregation's articles of incorporation in order to avoid unnecessary legal action.

6. Some councils successfully use a less formal setting for consulting the congregation. Names such as "town hall meeting" or "congregational forum" are used to describe these gatherings at which the council seeks congregational response to its planning and visioning.

44

SEARCHING FOR A NEW PASTOR

Your pastor accepted a call, you arranged a splendid farewell, and now you are without a pastor. You are "vacant"—an inelegant designation that church assemblies have avoided in their records.

What are the steps ahead of you? Here is a summary:

1. Your vacancy is a valuable time: talent can emerge and self-studies can be conducted.

2. Upon your request classis will appoint a counselor who will prove to be a valuable resource person (Church Order, art. 9).

3. Council appoints a search committee of ten to twelve members. At least one member should be an elder and one a deacon. The committee appoints a chairperson and two secretaries: one for keeping records and one for correspondence.

4. Rather than hurrying the calling process, the vacant church should take time to evaluate its present situation and determine its future course. The search committee is in a good position to initiate these studies and provide leadership. A series of consultations should be held with the council and the congregation.

Congregational questionnaires and research papers may facilitate this process. All this will help the congregation to decide on the type of gifts and interests the next pastor will need, and it will help the pastors with whom the committee negotiates to decide whether they are right for the job.

From these surveys and studies the search committee will prepare a comprehensive statement on vision, plans, and goals for the ministry of the church. This document will also help the committee to draft a job description for the new pastor. The committee should seek the support of the council at every point.

5. The search committee should contact the Ministerial Information Service (MIS) for a church profile questionnaire. Completing this form will help the committee to determine what kind of pastor the congregation needs. The studies mentioned above provide good input. The committee also should consult with the congregation and the council. The completed church profile should be returned to MIS.[1]

6. The committee prepares an information packet for the use of pastors who will be contacted. The packet should contain the statements mentioned in the pre-

vious sections and a brochure describing the congregation and surrounding community. Some churches also include a questionnaire for the pastors' use. The committee may also wish to enclose a copy of the MIS church profile.

7. Drawing up a list of names of pastors to consider is difficult. Sources for names include committee members, the counselor of classis, council members, and the congregation. You may also want to place an ad in the church papers. And you may ask MIS for names with matching profiles of pastors who may be able to consider a call.

8. Contact is made with the pastors on the committee's list by sending them the information packet. Individualized cover letters invite them to be part of the search process.

9. The committee studies and evaluates the responses, checks references, conducts telephone interviews, perhaps listens to sermon tapes, and reduces the long list to a short list. The committee may ask MIS for ministerial profiles of those on the short list. The short list is reduced to five names or so. In consultation with the council, these prospects may be invited for personal interviews and possibly for preaching. The church reimburses the pastors for expenses incurred.

10. The council considers the committee's recommendation and prepares a duo or a trio. Avoid single nominations. They reduce the congregation's input to virtually zero. In the case of a single nomination, voters may well show their displeasure by voting down the nomination. (See Church Order, art. 4.)

The council sets the date for the congregational meeting and informs the congregation. The committee provides profiles of each nominee to the members. Seek the advice of the classical counselor and be sure to have the counselor co-sign the letter of call.

11. Throughout the entire process the committee keeps the council and congregation informed and seeks their input.

12. As soon as pastors are no longer under consideration, they must be notified with expressions of appreciation.

13. The search committee, in consultation with the council, is in a good position to review the salary arrangement for the new pastor. Is the proposed salary adequate? Does the new pastor seem happy with it? Have moving expenses been considered? Has the new pastor incurred other miscellaneous expenses? Is the parsonage in good shape? Does the new pastor wish to receive a housing allowance instead of occupying the parsonage? Must budget adjustments be made?

Note

1. See also Louis M. Tamminga, *A New Pastor for Greensville,* a paper published by MIS, a division of CRC Pastoral Ministries, 2850 Kalamazoo Ave. SE, Grand Rapids, MI 49560.

45

OVERSEERS IN THE CHURCH

The designation "overseer" comes from Acts 20:28, which says, "Keep watch over yourselves and all the flock of which the Holy Spirit has made you overseers. Be shepherds of the church of God. . . ." 1 Peter 5:2 confirms it: "Be shepherds of God's flock that is under your care, serving as overseers. . . ."

What is involved in being an overseer?

1. Elders oversee each other. "Keep watch over yourselves." As a fellow elder the pastor assumes an active role in this oversight. (See also section 48.)

2. The elders are mandated to oversee the life and doctrine of the pastor(s). In the charge to the elders in the form for Ordination of Elders and Deacons we read, "Be wise counselors who support and strengthen the pastor." (See also section 49.)

The elders are expected to hold the pastor(s) to high standards of excellence. The elders must see to it that the pastors do their work with diligence, edification, and relevance, and that they walk in the Lord's ways.

The most important part of the pastor's task is the ministry of the Word and sacraments. The elders must see to it that the pastor is given ample time to prepare sermons. Preaching should be discussed regularly with the pastor(s) and always in a nonthreatening and nonjudgmental way. Pastors will appreciate helpful suggestions and hints. You should consider together whether sermons are

> We had come home from the morning service when our little son asked me, with a startled face, "Daddy, were the people in church really bad?" "No, no," I said, "why did you think they were?" "Oh," he said, "you yelled at them!"
>
> I should have known. Earlier an elder had said to me, "Give it to the congregation straight—repentance and forgiveness through the blood of the Lamb—but remember what you say from the pulpit and how you say it. Would you also put it to them that way at a family visit or even over lunch?"

balanced and relevant, are presented in an engaging manner and give evidence of careful preparation.

As is true for all professionals, local pastors should be given opportunity to upgrade their skills regularly by attending sermon workshops and seminars.

It is unrealistic to expect pastors to prepare two sermons every week and to maintain high quality. Elders should insist that pastors have a Sunday away from the pulpit occasionally. The week prior, the pastors can then catch up on visiting, studying, praying, planning, and administration.

Many councils appoint a small committee or perhaps designate the executive committee, to which the pastor reports regarding matters of ministry and preaching. This is also a good setting for consultation, suggestions, and feedback.

3. The elders must also oversee the congregation. Article 12a of the Church Order states, "[The pastor], with the elders, shall supervise the congregation." Article 25b is more detailed: "The elders, with the minister(s), shall oversee the doctrine and life of the members of the congregation and fellow officebearers, shall exercise admonition and discipline along with pastoral care in the congregation, shall participate in and promote evangelism, and shall defend the faith."

The form for Ordination of Elders and Deacons spells out similar details: "Elders are thus responsible for the spiritual well-being of God's people. They must provide true preaching and teaching, . . . and faithful counsel and discipline. . . . And they must promote fellowship and hospitality among believers, ensure good order in the church, and stimulate witness to all people."

4. The supervisory task of the elders extends also over the programmatic side of church life. The elders are responsible for such organized activities as church services, instruction classes, evangelism, church societies, and the meetings of the church and of the consistory. Also, elders should "diligently encourage the members of the congregation to establish and maintain good Christian schools" and to actively participate in organizations and institutions that promote God's kingdom. (See art. 71 and art. 72.)

The form states clearly that this governing task of the elders is spiritually conditioned. The Charge to the Elders includes these words: "Remember at all times that if you would truly give spiritual leadership in the household of faith, you must be completely mastered by your Lord."

46

EXERCISING DISCIPLINE

Accepting church membership means accepting its blessings and graces; it also means accepting its admonition and discipline. Nothing causes pastors and elders more agony in church life than the administration of discipline. In one short sentence the ordination form lays out the mandate: "Be compassionate, yet firm and consistent in rebuke and discipline."

The denomination itself has tried to help the churches in this difficult ministry. The entire fourth—and last—section of the Church Order is devoted to the ministry of discipline in the church. The synods of 1991 and 1992 adopted revisions of the fourth section of the Church Order. Those synods also adopted a set of guidelines for the churches' use. The forms to be used in the application of discipline were also amended. It is important for local councils to acquaint themselves with this helpful material. (See *Acts of Synod 1991,* p. 718 ff. and *Acts of Synod 1992,* p. 612.)

In the Church Order, the revised articles 78-81 guide the churches in the discipline of members; the revised articles 82-84 deal with the discipline of office-bearers.

In *The Manual of Christian Reformed Church Government* (1994), Richard R. De Ridder and Leonard J. Hofman list the following biblical references: Matthew 16:19; 18:15-17; 1 Corinthians 5:12-13; and 2 Corinthians 6:14-16. Also: the Belgic Confession, articles 29, 30, and 32, and the Heidelberg Catechism, Q&A's 82, 84-85. They also refer to the valuable study report on church discipline as printed in the *Acts of Synod 1976,* pp. 631-666. Pages 382-418 of the *Manual* contain a wealth of information of which councils should avail themselves.

Following is a summary of the principles and practices of the discipline ministry. It is by no means a substitute for studying the synodical documents in their entirety.

1. Discipline has one goal—to bring people back to God. Discipline is much like "discipling," which means to acquaint people with Jesus so they will become his followers. Restoring erring members to a living church membership is what discipline is all about.

2. Discipline is part of the pastoral ministry of the church. All members need it, since all members are sinners. No one can flourish in the faith without correction. Members are responsible for each other—they should discipline each other long before formal discipline by the elders begins. Correction is part of the gospel message. In fact, discipline

begins with me. I must discipline myself. I am accountable to God and to my fellow believers. Elders may point this out to members who live in disobedience—they ought to engage in self-discipline.

3. Elders struggle with the question of when to proceed with formal discipline. Is every sin censurable? Potentially, yes; in practice, no. The degree to which the sin is practiced is a factor. Public offense is a factor. The attitude of the sinner is probably the biggest factor. If the offender persists, shows no repentance, and will not acknowledge the particular sin, then after repeated pleadings, formal censure begins.

4. The churches have agreed to a uniform course of action designed to be fair to the offending member and to restore him or her to full membership in the church community. The process begins with a visit, followed (probably) by several more. Two elders invite the member to explain the offense. They discuss the issue thoroughly, thoughtfully, and prayerfully. Unless the member acknowledges his or her sin at this point, the elders will inform the member that they will report the visit to the consistory and seek its counsel.

The consistory takes careful note of the elders' report and must decide whether it considers the sin worthy of censure. If it does, another visit will be made. Again the elders will try to bring the member to acknowledge the sin and repent of it. If they are unsuccessful, the consistory must decide whether to proceed with discipline. If it does, it will inform the member through the visiting elders that he or she is barred from the Lord's Supper. Other membership privileges are also suspended.

Bert did not have a good reputation in the congregation I served as a pastor. He was given to anger and harsh criticism. People intuitively avoided Bert.

At one of our elders' meetings prior to the Lord's Supper, an elder reported that he had it on good authority that Bert had accused another elder (who was present) of a serious wrongdoing in his past. Silence hung heavily on the assembly. The elder who reported this then proposed that Bert be visited and be told not to partake of the Lord's Supper.

There was another painful silence. Then the elder against whom Bert had made the accusation spoke quietly. "Bert and I grew up in the same village," he said. "Bert's family had many problems and suffered a lot. Bert's own family has a lot of problems, too, and he has a hard time in the mill where he works. With your permission I will see Bert tonight."

And so the elder left the meeting to visit with Bert. We prayed together for the Lord's guidance. After an hour the elder returned. He told the elders that the problem had been resolved, the wrong explained, confessed, and forgiven. He also said that on behalf of the elders he had invited Bert to participate in the Lord's Supper that Sunday.

None of these actions—sometimes called "silent censure"—are reported to the congregation.

5. Normally, pastoral visits continue for some time as the elders attempt to bring the member to repentance. If they are unsuccessful, they will report to the consistory again, and more discussion and prayers follow. The consistory must then decide whether to proceed with the next stage of censure, sometimes called "public censure."

The visiting elders call on the member again and inform him or her that an announcement will be made in an upcoming worship service that a brother or sister of the congregation refuses to repent of a certain sin and that the congregation will be asked to pray for him or her. This is the first step of public censure. The member remains anonymous, and the nature of the sin is not divulged.

6. In the meantime, pastoral visits continue. If the member remains unrepentant, the consistory will decide whether to take the second step of public censure. This step consists of an announcement to the congregation that the member has not repented and will be excommunicated from the church fellowship on a predetermined date if he or she remains unrepentant.

Before the consistory takes this step, it must consult with classis and receive its endorsement. Also, well before the announcement is made, the elders will visit the member again, plead with him or her to repent, and explain all the details of the step the council intends to take. If the member has no change of heart, the announcement is made on the appointed Sunday.

The announcement contains

a. A request to the congregation to pray for the member. (The member's name is revealed, but the nature of the sin is not. *Acts of Synod 1991*, pp. 720-722.)
b. The date at which the member will be excluded from the membership unless repentance occurs.

7. If possible the elders will visit again before the date of excommunication. If this is fruitless, the consistory will proceed with excommunication. The final announcement to that effect will be made to the congregation. The form for Excommunication in the back of the *Psalter Hymnal* may be read.

8. Excommunication does not relieve the consistory from providing ongoing pastoral care, if possible. Sometimes a person who has been confronted with this extreme action will repent and be readmitted as a member. In fact, article 81d asks the consistory to "inform the congregation and encourage its involvement in both the exclusion from and the readmission to membership." The consistory may ask its evangelism committee to seek out these people.

9. In this age of high mobility it sometimes happens that members move away without informing the council regarding their church membership. Synod drafted

the following guideline—"that baptized or confessing members who move away from the area of their church so that a meaningful church relationship is no longer possible, may retain their membership in their home church at their request and with the consent of the consistory. If they fail to make such a request and do not transfer to a church near them, the consistory, having made serious attempts to rectify the situation, may declare their membership lapsed after a period of two years from the date of their departure. The member concerned shall be notified by the consistory of its action if at all possible" (Supplement to Church Order art. 67, *Church Order/ Rules for Synodical Procedure 1997*, p. 70).

10. Formal discipline of baptized members who have not made public profession of faith is simpler than that of full members. When such a member neglects the services of the Lord or becomes delinquent in doctrine or life, the consistory, after repeated admonitions, will inform the member of its intention to terminate his or her membership in the church.

The consistory must seek the approval of classis. An announcement is made to the congregation that on a certain date the member will be excluded from the church unless he or she repents. None of these steps are taken without several pastoral visits having been made.

11. In many cases those under discipline will resign their membership before the process is completed. Synod advised the following: ". . . those who do this, should be earnestly and continually admonished to return from their error, and should not be quickly let go; but also that always also the joining the Church as institute, and remaining with it, canonically must remain to each one freely, therefore judges that a person can no longer be an object of discipline, if he persists in resigning his membership" (*Acts of Synod 1918*, p. 66). The congregation shall be informed accordingly. Be sure to keep careful written records of all proceedings.[1]

Note
1. See also Harry G. Arnold, *Discipline in the Church* (Grand Rapids, Mich.: CRC Publications, 1989).

DISCIPLINE OF OFFICEBEARERS

One of the saddest tasks that a council is ever called to do is to discipline one of its own members: a minister, elder, deacon, or evangelist.

Most circumstances surrounding the discipline of officebearers are complex, and councils may not know how to proceed. They would do well to call in the classical church visitors for advice early in the process. When the pastor is involved, the council may turn to the denomination's Pastor-Church Relations Services (PCRS) or to PCRS's regional pastor in the classis.

Following is a summary of denominational guidelines for the discipline of officebearers:

1. Articles 82-84 of the Church Order deal with the discipline of officebearers.[1] Censurable offenses by officebearers are generally committed in the following areas: violations of the Form of Subscription, neglect or abuse of office, or serious deviations from sound doctrine and godly conduct (art. 83).

2. The church distinguishes between general discipline and special discipline of officebearers. General discipline applies to them in their role as members of the church. Special discipline applies to them in their role as officebearers.

General discipline is not to be applied until special discipline has been initiated. When repentance has been expressed during the process of special discipline, general discipline is usually not applied, even when an officebearer is ultimately deposed from the office.

3. Special discipline begins with temporarily suspending officebearers from the duties and privileges of office. At this stage the officebearers have not yet been found guilty. The judicial process that follows is thus not encumbered by the tasks the officebearers have pledged to do.

The council suspending the accused officebearer must seek the concurrence of the nearest Christian Reformed council. If the two councils disagree, the matter goes to classis for resolution. Suspension then takes effect when classis has approved the first council's action.

4. If the ensuing judicial process establishes the officebearer's guilt and if this would lead to the officebearer's genuine repentance, the council may lift the suspension. The council may also decide to depose the officebearer if it judges that the past sin would hamper further service. Councils can restore suspended officebearers to service only when

doing so would glorify God and benefit the church (art. 84).

5. The deposition of a minister of the Word requires the approval of the classis of which the local church is part. Classis shall make its decision with the concurring advice of the synodical deputies of the three neighboring classes. The actual deposition is done by the minister's council. The stated clerk of classis must inform the other classes in the denomination of the deposition, each of whom must inform the clerks of the councils of the churches.

6. When a minister resigns from office because of having fallen into some sin or while under discipline, the church council must continue the procedures as outlined in articles 82-84 of the Church Order. In general, the council must make a disposition of the status of a minister who resigns. It must declare which of the following four conditions prevails:

a. The resigned minister is honorably released.
b. The resigned minister is released.
c. The resigned minister is dismissed.

What do officebearers agree to when they sign the Form of Subscription?

By signing the form, officebearers declare that they subscribe without reservation to the doctrines contained in the confessions of the church (the Belgic Confession, the Canons of Dort, and the Heidelberg Catechism) as being taught in the Word of God.

Though the confessions are human formulations and are not equal to Scripture, the church ascribes a high level of authority to them. Disagreement with the confessions can lead to disciplinary action.

Synod formulated guidelines for officebearers to follow in cases of disagreement with a creedal doctrine. An individual officebearer may file a "confessional-difficulty gravamen" (a grievance petition) by which a personal difficulty with the confession is expressed, or a "confessional-disagreement gravamen" by which a subscriber makes recommendations for a revision of the creeds.

Synod qualified the scope of the creeds' authority somewhat by stating that "a subscriber does not by his subscription declare that these doctrines are all stated in the best possible manner, or . . . cover all that the Scriptures teach on the matters confessed . . . nor . . . that every teaching of the Scriptures is set forth in our confessions. . . ."

Synod added that a subscriber is "not bound to the references, allusions, and remarks that are incidental to the formulation of these doctrines nor to the theological deductions" (Supplement to Church Order art. 5, *Church Order/Rules for Synodical Procedure 1997*, p. 25-26).

d. The resigned minister is in the status of one deposed.[2]

When ministers, guilty of a censurable sin, resign their membership in the CRC, the formal disciplinary process is discontinued. The disposition as outlined above must then still be made.

7. A deposed minister may make application toward readmission to office. The decision to declare such a minister eligible for a call is to be made by the classis in which the deposition took place. The concurring advice of the three synodical deputies is required (art. 84).

Notes

1. See also *Acts of Synod 1991,* pp. 719-720.
2. See Church Order, article 14b and its supplement.

48

MUTUAL ENCOURAGEMENT AND ACCOUNTABILITY

The work of an officebearer is demanding. Not only the volume but the gravity of the work demands that officebearers always encourage one another. The form states that elders should be "wise counselors who support and strengthen the pastor." In return, the pastor will "support and strengthen" the officebearers, and they will do so to each other (2 Thess. 2:13-17).

How can officebearers encourage each other?

1. They should intentionally take an interest in one another as persons and in one another's ministry. Such interest should be expressed in thoughtful words and graceful gestures. Perhaps you are aware of a problem or a burden in the life of a fellow council member. Talk with that person about it.

2. Consult together, especially in difficult pastoral matters. Don't hesitate to seek the advice of a trusted colleague on council.

3. Cultivate interpersonal relationships. Good relationships are basic to constructive council work.

4. Adopt a prayer discipline that includes specific petitions for your colleagues on council. Don't neglect communal prayers.

5. Church Order article 36b stipulates that at least quarterly the council "shall exercise mutual censure, which concerns the performance of the official duties of the officebearers." Taken literally, this article proposes that council members individually declare that they approve of one another's work and walk of life.

Councils often do mutual censure (also called "censura morum") in their meeting before the Lord's Supper. When done thoughtfully this practice can be very helpful, especially when the officebearers seriously evaluate the quality of the council's work. The bottom line is that officebearers should deal with misgivings without delay and on a personal level. If that does not solve the problems, they should seek the advice of council. Elders, deacons, and ministers, in other words, agree to be accountable to each other.

This article also implies that councils should regularly set aside time to evaluate the quality of their ministry and the well-being of the congregation. Can improvements be made? Can new initiatives be taken? Councils should also periodically thank God for the privilege of serving together as colleagues in a spirit of friendship and mutual appreciation.

Councils, then, must put on the mind of Christ and accept Paul's benediction from 2 Thessalonians 2:16-17: "May our Lord Jesus Christ himself and God our Father, who loved us and by his grace gave us eternal encouragement and good hope, encourage your hearts and strengthen you in every good deed and word."

49

SUPPORTING THE MINISTER

The demands made on the time and energy of ministers are probably more than the congregation and the council realize. Take just one real-life example: a young member of the church was found to have used and sold drugs. The distraught parents phoned the minister who subsequently joined a team of professional caregivers. Over the next six weeks the minister's log showed twelve visits and conferences: three with the parents, four with their son, one with the school guidance counselor, two with the therapist who was brought in, one with the principal, and one with a court official.

The minister had to adjust his schedule to make some of these visits. They all were emotionally draining, and the minister did not feel at liberty to inform the council of these time investments.

Is this an exceptional situation? Probably. Remember, though, that ministers regularly face exceptional situations.

What can elders do to support their ministers?

1. Ministers are shepherds, not hirelings. They do not seek sympathy, but they value understanding and expressions of appreciation. It means a lot to ministers

when elders are aware of the weight of their responsibilities.

2. Elders and deacons should see to it that ministers' salaries are commensurate with the demands of their office. Compensation should be discussed annually in a setting of trust and frankness.

3. Ministers have an open-ended job. The boundaries between private life and professional life can easily be blurred. Elders can help ministers to keep the two areas distinct and can encourage the minister to live wholeheartedly in each.

4. In view of the demands on their time and energy, ministers tend not to read, study, and reflect as much as they should. Elders should insist that ministers take periodic study leaves and sabbaticals, and plan time each week for reading and replenishment.

5. Ministers need regular relief from preaching. Those weeks when they need not prepare sermons will be used for catching up on visiting, administration, and teaching preparation.

6. The elders are not only shepherds to the members but also to the ministers. They should discuss with the ministers how pastoral care can best be provided

to them. The ministers' spiritual and emotional health should not be taken for granted.

Synod has often expressed its concern for the well-being of ministers and staff. In 1982 Synod proposed that local churches set up a support group for each of their ministry personnel (*Acts of Synod 1982,* p. 78).

Not every church has acted upon this advice, but those who have have found it a good provision of additional and consistent care for pastors. These so-called pastoral relations committees are usually composed of three members: an elder and two congregational members, one male and one female. They are chosen in consultation with the pastor and spouse for their wisdom, maturity, discretion, and godliness. They meet with the pastor-couple at least once a month for prayer and encouragement. As in all pastoral caregiving, the support group does its work in strict confidentiality.

Note

For advice and resource materials contact the office of Pastor-Church Relations, 2850 Kalamazoo Ave. SE, Grand Rapids, MI 49560. Call 616-224-0746.

COMMUNICATION

Good communication is the oil that lubricates the church machinery. Without effective communication, commendable initiatives may come to naught.

Following are some considerations:

1. Council must assure that a well-functioning communication system is in place. Such a system provides for a smooth information flow from council to congregation and from congregation to council, and, generally, keeps members informed about congregational activities.

An effective communication system doesn't just happen. It must be designed and tended. The advantages of such a system are many. Members will relate to the church better when they know what goes on, what programs are available, and what challenges are met. They also want to know what their council is doing and why.

2. Church bulletins have become effective communication devices. Many churches also publish a newsletter containing information regarding the church's programs. The production of these media deserves the full cooperation of council members, committee secretaries, and others who contribute information. Promptness, brevity, and accuracy are always appreciated.

3. Pastors, elders, and deacons must keep each other informed. Paul advises in Acts 20:28 to "keep watch over . . . all the flock." You should know what is going on in the congregation. Be each other's eyes and ears and share pertinent observations with the proper officebearer.

4. Communication must be marked by honesty and integrity. There will be victories and defeats. The congregation will grow from knowing that fellow members have shed tears.

VISIONING, PLANNING, GOAL SETTING, AND PROGRAMMING

Most members assume some parts of a congregation's ministry are "givens"—church services are held, pastoral care is offered, classes are taught, and a variety of societies and committees meet. This has been true for generations, and it will be true for years to come. These basic elements are exceedingly durable.

In recent times, churches have looked carefully at what is unique about their convictions, gifts, needs, interests, resources, and skills, and how those characteristics fit with the challenges of their members and community. They ask, who are we, why are we here, and what is our calling?

This has been a good development. Churches began to search the Scriptures for answers and their hearts for obedient responses.

A new terminology made its entry among the churches when leaders spoke of vision statements, mission statements, master planning, goal setting, prioritizing, self studies, congregational surveys, monitoring progress and change, and so on.

Has your church done comprehensive planning? If so, is the vision statement still relevant? Has your council done its share to implement the plans that the congregation agreed upon? Have you

carefully assessed progress? Have you interacted constructively with those who led the master-planning process? Have some of the goals been reached? Have you kept the congregation informed? Have necessary corrections and adjustments been made?

In order to answer these questions, your council may set aside a Saturday or weekday evening to consult with the leadership team. If your church has not done such vision study and planning, consider doing so.[1] The advantages are many. You will involve the members in searching the Scriptures regarding the nature and calling of the church. Members will be challenged to discover their gifts and to use them in the Lord's service. You will probably discover some real talent among your members, and you will help them to discern needs in your church's neighborhood that they are equipped to meet. Most importantly, your church may win people for the Lord and provide them with a wonderful church home.

Note

1. See Dirk J. Hart, *Charting a Course for Your Church* and *New Designs for Ministry Structure* (Grand Rapids, Mich.: CRC Publications, 1996). Christian Reformed Home Missions is available to assist you in comprehensive ministry planning. Call toll-free 1-800-266-2175.

RELATING TO CHURCH STAFF

Almost all CRC churches employ secretarial and administrative personnel, and more than half have additional church staff workers. In order for a church to profit from the services of its staff, consider the following observations:

1. You have appointed your staff people for their professional skills and vision. Grant them every professional courtesy. Hold them in the highest esteem.

2. Each staff person should have a contract agreed upon between him or her and the council. All conditions of employment should be carefully spelled out and clearly understood.

3. Each staff person should have a job description. Job descriptions should be regularly consulted and fine-tuned as necessary.

4. Internal staff relationships are very important. The staff should meet once a week for prayer, planning, reporting, and mutual accountability. Differences should not be allowed to go unresolved.

5. Staffs have been found to function best when there is a staff head. This person should coordinate and integrate staff activities and be its main spokesperson to council. The staff head will see to it that all major planning and decision-making is done by staff consensus. No new ministry projects should be initiated without broad staff backing.

6. Councils should appoint a small staff committee from its members to supervise the staff and serve as staff liaison to council.

7. The staff should submit a written report of its work and vision to the council. Individual staff members should be given the courtesy to attend council meetings as resource persons. When their part of the report is discussed, they should have the privilege of the floor.

8. Communication between individual staff people and between staff and council is important. The staff head will give this careful attention.[1]

Note

1. See also Dirk J. Hart, *Staffing the Established Church* (Grand Rapids, Mich.: CRC Publications, 1993) and Louis M. Tamminga, *Questions Church Staffs Ask* (Grand Rapids, Mich.: CRC Pastor-Church Relations).

DEALING WITH CHANGE

Growth always creates change. A vigorous church program will produce its share of necessary changes. Changes are not always welcomed by church members and leaders. Change is often uncomfortable. However, without it, church life will stagnate. The early years of the sixteenth-century Reformation produced incredible growth, but people had to cope with profound changes.

Here are some things to keep in mind:

1. Change for the sake of change is unhelpful. Opposing all change is bad too. You as a council must determine, with an open mind, which changes should be accepted courageously and which should be countered. Explain your policy to the congregation.

2. Have you made thorough preparations? Do you understand the proposed ministry that will bring changes? Do you have the necessary resources? Are those in charge skilled to see it through? Has the congregation been duly informed? You can cope confidently with change if you are convinced that you are on course.

3. Resistance to change often creates secondary problems with their own complexities. You may reassure the congregation that the old foundations have

not crumbled, but don't backpedal under pressure. Spell out your good hopes for the ministries under fire.

4. Consistency is essential. Once you have agreed on a certain program and

Some years ago I spent a weekend with a church in California for an elders' workshop and a congregational retreat. Though this church made no secret of its conservative stance, the worship services were unusually innovative and vibrant.

Later I remarked about it to a senior elder. He said, "It is a team effort. The whole congregation is involved, but much of the credit goes to our pastor. He made both council and congregation study the biblical principles of worship. Our pastor always consults the council. We regularly evaluate the services. So we keep on learning and improving. The pastor is always well prepared. He leads the order of worship with respect and dignity. And he insists that those who participate in the liturgy do the same."

given those in charge your blessing, you cannot, as a council, go into hiding when opposition becomes vocal. You must stay the course and inform the congregation accordingly.

5. Maintain a balanced program of ministry. For example, you may agree to introduce a new type of song into worship, but assure the congregation that you will continue to treasure seasoned hymnody as well.

6. Monitor change. As council members and leaders, review ministry programs and practices regularly. Make corrections and adjustments as necessary.

7. Good taste is important. See to it that things are done in a churchly manner. Worship services, especially, have to be conducted in an edifying way. (See section 54.)

54

DEALING WITH CONFLICT

Few churches are spared the anguish of congregational conflicts. The issues and dynamics surrounding such conflict are usually very complex. Dealing with conflict and working toward resolution is one of the hardest parts of the parish ministry.

Conflicts between parties that have dug in for battle can rarely be resolved without outside help. For that reason, the following brief observations will need to be augmented by competent resource people along the way.

Suppose you and a fellow elder have agreed to assist some of your members in finding their way out of a conflict situation. What are some of the things to keep in mind?

1. Unresolved conflicts grow. The longer they last, the more difficult resolution becomes. Such conflicts are bound to affect the entire congregation.

2. The two parties in the conflict (each of which may comprise a cluster of members) must agree to your ministry to them. It must be clearly understood that your offer of help has been accepted by everyone involved.

3. The preparatory stage of your efforts is important. Visit with one party at a time. Go back and forth between the two. Gently remind the parties that you are not a miracle worker and that their cooperation is a key factor in arriving at a resolution. Assure them also that if all parties earnestly seek reconciliation, they should expect that it will happen.

4. Each party will invariably be convinced of the rightness of its cause. Each wants to come out as the winner in the contest. Point out that justice is important to you, but that reconciliation can only be the result of conceding points, accepting explanations, letting go of presumed bad motives, and honoring assurances of good faith.

5. Be charitable and sympathetic toward all the participants. They have not become embroiled in this conflict by bad intent. They probably feel threatened and hurt by events over which they may have had no control. If you find it difficult to like them as persons, it is because they are in bondage to fear and anger. Be patient with them. Don't allow their fear and anger to rub off on you.

6. Know the facts. As you visit with each of the parties, try to determine what the contested issues are. Do both parties give the same account? Who is involved? Ongoing conflicts tend to draw in bystanders. How high is the anger level?

Is it clear what the combatants demand from each other? As you interview the parties, do some probing. Give them feedback. What exactly is each one saying? Why are they saying it? If you see inconsistencies and discrepancies, follow up on them in a nonthreatening way.

7. Before you get the two parties around the bargaining table, resolve that you will take only a small step at a time. Conflicts are rarely solved quickly. (If they are, they will probably flare up again.) Your clients hold deep feelings and strong perceptions: they will not yield readily. Before you can hope to resolve a conflict, you must contain it. That is a small victory.

8. Now the hard part: conducting a face-to-face meeting of the parties. If you have found during the preparatory stage that anger and hurt run very deep, you may suggest bringing in some skilled mediators. But before you do so, make sure the idea has the approval of both parties and the church council. The parties may initially oppose the idea. Point out, patiently, that they have to face reality: their conflict is serious and, unless resolved, will do great harm to themselves, to their children, and to the congregation.

9. Begin the bargaining meeting with welcome and prayer. Briefly state the purpose of the meeting. Make an appeal for everyone's goodwill and cooperation.

Next, spell out the ground rules. Point out that you are in charge of the meeting. Anyone who wishes to speak must first be recognized by you. You cannot allow interruptions. Common courtesy is expected of all. The participants have to understand that this is not the last meeting. You will propose further meetings as needed. State also that you as mediators have pledged yourselves to impartiality and fairness. Explain that this is not a court session at which verdicts are laid down. This is a meeting of reconciliation at which followers of Christ strive to overcome their differences and accept one another as members of Christ's body.

10. Now read a carefully prepared statement about the nature of the conflict, the issues at stake, and perhaps a summary of how the conflict developed. You may also refer to previous meetings with the individual parties.

Invite the participants to respond. Allow ample time to go over details even though you see little progress. Keep the discussions on track. Appeal to the parties to accept each other's explanations as sincere. Do not allow anyone to ascribe bad motives to anyone else. Do not allow angry outbursts and harsh accusations, but do allow anger to surface. If there appears to be some reason for anger, ask the opposing party to respond. If the response is even remotely positive, summarize it in your own words. Try to be the catalyst for the parties to offer clarifications, explanations, and assurances of goodwill. See whether misunderstandings and misinterpretations can be removed. Solicit responses when that happens.

11. This stage of the process is very unpredictable. Don't hesitate to announce a brief recess to consult together as mediators. If the meeting has gone well, draft a statement of explanations and conclusions, sit down with the leaders of each party separately, and see what it takes for them to give their initial fiat. Then call the meeting to order again, and negotiate the acceptance of the statement as a basis for resolution and reconciliation.

If it appears that another session is necessary, inform the participants of this in a charitable way, impressing upon them the need to refrain from further action and talk that could set the process back. Careful records should be kept of the sessions and proceedings.

12. When reconciliation has been reached, a modest form of celebration can be helpful. Perhaps the parties will agree to come together, shake hands, and assure one another of goodwill and acceptance. Prayers and songs can be part of such a session. Decide whether a statement should be made to the congregation. If you think it advisable, get the approval of the parties.

13. Follow-up care is vital. The parties need to be visited and assured of God's grace. Ongoing expressions of fear need to be addressed in personal visits. The pastor, especially, can play a wholesome role in this effort.[1]

Note
1. CRC Pastor-Church Relations in Grand Rapids is prepared to assist the churches in this type of ministry. See also Louis M. Tamminga, *Conflict in the Church* (Grand Rapids, Mich.: CRC Publications, 1988). Further resources include Speed B. Leas, *Moving Your Church Through Conflict* (Washington, D.C.: Alban Institute, Inc., 1985), and Robert D. Dale, *Surviving Difficult Church Members* (Nashville: Abingdon Press, 1984).

55

OVERSEEING THE WORSHIP SERVICES

Worship services are the pillars of the church's ministry program. Nothing contributes so much to congregational health and growth as preaching and worship. What can elders do in this very demanding area of church life?

Be aware of some of the basic provisions in the Church Order regarding worship services.

You are in charge: "The consistory shall regulate the worship services" (art. 52a). Synod affirmed the "rich tradition of assembling for worship twice on the Lord's Day" (art. 51 supplement). Prominent elements in the service are preaching, sacraments, praise, prayer, and offerings. Synodically approved Bible versions and hymnals shall be used. The same holds for liturgical forms. Worship services are to be conducted by ministers who must "explain and apply Holy Scripture" (art. 54a). In case of "reading services" the council must approve the sermons. The Heidelberg Catechism shall ordinarily be used in the preaching every Sunday (art. 51-54).

Synods, generally, have been concerned about preserving uniformity among the churches in liturgical practices. More recently, however, synods have recognized the need for diversity and spontaneity in worship and have allowed councils a degree of flexibility (*Acts of Synod 1970*, p. 69; *Acts of Synod 1991*, pp. 706-707).

In worship, believers meet communally before God who is present in his Word, Spirit, and grace. An extraordinary dialogue takes place: God and his children address each other and respond to each other. Some of the acts on God's part are the preaching (through a designated servant), the liturgical reading of his will, the assurance of pardon for sin, and the blessings pronounced upon the congregation. Some of the acts on the part of the congregation are confession of sin, prayer, singing, praise, offering, surrender, and listening and responding to the preaching. In the sacraments both God and the worshiping community speak and act in concert.

The preaching is a prominent element in the worship service. In it the Word is explained and proclaimed, the kingdom is announced, the salvation of Christ is proclaimed, and the congregation is summoned to repentance, faith, and obedience. God's people are established in their covenantal walk with God and are equipped for service. Worship is an end in itself and also a means to an end.

The elders should see to it that elements of the liturgy that do not contribute to this mutual engagement between God and his people are not given a prominent place in worship.

1. Preparation for the services is important. Many churches now have a worship committee that assists in preparing the services. This has much potential for good. Services are communal; preparations deserve to be made communally as well. There is much to be learned. Don't be upset when mistakes are made, as long as those involved learn from them. The pastor(s) will be part of this process. It may, initially, take some extra time to work with a team instead of doing it the old, trusted solo way. But all will benefit in the end.

2. Be aware of the seasons of the church year such as Epiphany, Lent, Easter, Pentecost, and Advent. The tone and mood of the services are affected by the salvation foci of these seasons. Remember also that specific congregational experiences may call for services that range from celebration to lament.

3. Singing is an important element in the services. Synod said "stick with approved songs" (as in the *Psalter Hymnal)* and added that when supplementary hymns are used, the synodical regulations governing hymns and anthems be observed.

Elders, pastors, and liturgical committee members should develop spiritual and theological antennae to assure excellence in congregational music and singing. Helpful summaries of principles that can guide them in this endeavor can be found in the blue *Psalter Hymnal*, page v, and the gray *Psalter Hymnal*, pages 11-15. They deserve careful study. The four liturgical motifs listed in the Statement of Principle in the gray hymnal are that church music should be biblical, catholic, confessional, and pastoral. Note also that the "music of the church should be appropriate for worship— that is, it should be liturgical and have aesthetic integrity."

4. Congregational prayer deserves careful preparation. It is a unique event in which the entire congregation assembles for supplication and intercession. Prayers should reflect the focus of the preaching and worship service, the needs and challenges of the congregation, and the needs and conditions of the world. The intercessory element should never be absent from congregational prayers.

5. The elders should encourage the minister(s) to devote significant time to worship preparation. From time to time they should review the services and give the minister(s) the benefit of their constructive suggestions. Those would also be choice moments to study the principles for worship, music, and songs.

Note

Helpful worship study reports are found in *Acts of Synod 1928,* pp. 276-302; *Acts of Synod 1930,* pp. 335-353; and *Acts of Synod 1968,* pp. 134-198. Worship leaders will benefit from *Reformed Worship*—a periodical for music and liturgy published quarterly by CRC Publications, 2850 Kalamazoo Ave. SE, Grand Rapids, MI 49560. See also James A. DeJong, *Into His Presence* (Grand Rapids, Mich.: CRC Publications, 1985).

56

OVERSEEING THE ADMINISTRATION OF THE SACRAMENTS

The sacraments—the Lord's Supper and baptism—are essential parts of the worship service. They eminently fit the dialogue pattern described in the previous chapter. In holy communion God offers himself sacramentally to the congregation, and the congregation eats and drinks in belief. In baptism the water symbolizes and seals the grace of God in Jesus Christ. The persons baptized (or their parents) and the entire congregation believingly accept and pledge to live productive Christian lives.

What can the elders do to enhance the celebration of the sacraments? Following is a summary of the denomination's understanding of the sacraments.

Both sacraments

Articles 55-60 of the Church Order deal with the sacraments.

The prescribed forms shall be used with the sacraments; adaptations are permitted when conforming to synodical guidelines (art. 55; *Acts of Synod 1991*, pp. 706-707; *Agenda for Synod 1994*, pp. 166-191).

The sacraments are administered upon the authority of the consistory in a public worship service by a minister of the Word or by an evangelist. Word and sacrament belong together (art. 55).

Baptism

1. "The covenant of God shall be sealed to children of believers by holy baptism. The consistory shall see to it that baptism is requested and administered as soon as feasible" (art. 56).

2. "Members who . . . fail to present their children for baptism should be instructed and admonished patiently, and if this proves ineffective, they should be disciplined" (*Acts of Synod 1888*, p. 19).

3. Children adopted by believing parents may be baptized (*Acts of Synod 1930*, p. 93).

4. "Adults who have not been baptized shall receive holy baptism upon public profession of faith. The form for the Baptism of Adults shall be used for such public professions" (art. 57).

5. Synod disapproved of rebaptism of adults, stating that such practice "is not in accord with the teaching of Scripture and the confession . . ." (*Acts of Synod 1971*, p. 162).

6. Synod urged parents to be faithful in explaining to their children the meaning and implications of infant baptism (*Acts of Synod 1973*, p. 78).

7. "The baptism of one who comes from another Christian denomination shall be held valid if it has been administered in the name of the triune God, by someone authorized by that denomination" (art. 58).

8. For your own orientation see the forms for baptism in the *Psalter Hymnal.* Also Lord's Days 25-27 of the Heidelberg Catechism; and Belgic Confession, art. 33 and 34; and *Our World Belongs to God,* sec. 40.

9. Synod rejected baptism with the Holy Spirit as a "second blessing" with an appeal to 1 Corinthians 12:13: "For we were all baptized by one Spirit into one body . . . and were all given the one Spirit to drink." Synod also referred to Ephesians 2:18; 2:22; John 3:5; Acts 2:39; Romans 8:1-17; 15:13; 1 Corinthians 3:16; 2 Corinthians 1:21; Galatians 3:2; 5:16-26; and 1 John 2:20-27.

Synod urged the churches to examine themselves with regard to the painful lack of religious assurance and of appreciation for a full-fledged covenantal life in Christ. Synod stated that both in the proclamation and reception of salvation the work of the Holy Spirit is indispensable (*Acts of Synod 1973,* p. 73).

The Lord's Supper

1. "The Lord's Supper shall be administered at least once every three months. The consistory shall provide for such administrations as it shall judge most conducive to edification. However, the ceremonies as prescribed in God's Word shall not be changed" (art. 60). Synod encouraged the churches to celebrate

the supper more often than once every three months (*Acts of Synod 1971,* p. 131; see also the Belgic Confession, art. 35, and the Heidelberg Catechism Lord's Days 28-30).

The Sacrament of the Lord's Supper

We believe that our good God,
mindful of our crudeness and weakness, has ordained sacraments for us
  to seal his promises in us,
  to pledge his good will and grace toward us,
  and also to nourish and sustain our faith . . .

. . . confirming in us
the salvation he imparts to us . . .

. . . although the manner in which he does it goes beyond our understanding
and is incomprehensible to us . . .

. . . yet we do not go wrong when we say
that what is eaten is Christ's own natural body
and what is drunk is his own blood—
but the manner in which we eat it
is not by the mouth but by the Spirit,
  through faith.

—from the Belgic Confession,
articles 33 and 35

2. Method and ways of supervision of the supper is left to the consistory (*Acts of Synod 1975,* p. 103).

3. Guests who are communicant members in good standing of a Christian

church may be invited to partake but should be informed of the requirements for participation: repentance, faith, and obedient living (*Acts of Synod 1975*, p. 103).

4. The sick may receive the Lord's Supper at home with a representation of the congregation (*Acts of Synod 1914*, p. 17).

5. Those who persevere in the negligence of the supper become subject to discipline (*Acts of Synod 1904*, p. 38).

6. May children attend the Lord's Supper? Yes, upon "an appropriate examination concerning their motives, faith, and life" before their public profession of faith. When those who have made that profession reach eighteen years of age they shall be invited to make a further commitment to the creeds of the Christian Reformed Church and the responsibilities of adult membership and be accorded the full rights and privileges of such membership (*Acts of Synod 1995*, p. 762; art. 59b).

The sacraments were given by Christ to the church for strengthening the faith of the believers. It is the gospel itself that brings the message of salvation and by God's grace changes hearts. The sacraments are instituted by the Lord to portray and seal these realities of salvation. In that sense, the sacraments are an added gift: what the gospel promises, the sacraments confirm in a visible, tangible way. Christ gave the sacraments, basically, because we are slow learners and are easily discouraged.

Isn't it embarrassing that Christians over the centuries were so bitterly divided over the sacraments—these extra special gifts of Christ to comfort the faint-hearted—that they fought wars over them and divided churches over them? The disputes were never fully settled because the Word of God does not give many details about the sacraments. The Lord's love-gift came with a minimum of explanation.

In response, your consistory can do at least two things:

- Teach the congregation to be grateful for the riches of the sacraments and to use them in faith and reverence. For example, the Lord's Supper is more than a memorial; it is a "spiritual table at which Christ communicates himself to us with all his benefits" (Belgic Confession, art. 35).

- Head off any disputes over the meaning and practice of the sacraments. Is that easier said than done? Perhaps, but avoid sanctioning certain details of the celebration at the exclusion of others claiming biblical backing for it.

USING THE HEIDELBERG CATECHISM IN PREACHING

Our churches have said, through their synods, "Use the catechism—regularly and systematically."

Article 54b of the Church Order says, "At one of the services each Lord's Day, the minister shall ordinarily preach the Word as summarized in the Heidelberg Catechism, following its sequence."

Note some implications:

1. The word "ordinarily" is used to avoid rigidity. Exceptions may be made occasionally.

2. Note the phrase "in sequence." Don't skip through the Heidelberg at random. Go through it systematically.

3. Note also that the phrase "preach the catechism" does not appear in the Church Order. The catechism is a (incomplete) summary and interpretation of the Word of God, a human formulation that is not equal to the Word. The Word is preached; the preaching is aided by the catechism.

4. There are at least two advantages to using the catechism regularly.

   a. It helps the preachers deal with the main themes of salvation as the catechism gleans them from the Word. Thus it keeps preachers from becoming one-sided, dwelling too much on their own choices as to what is important.

   b. The catechism has helped to create in the churches a common understanding of the doctrines of salvation and the godly walk of life. Synod suggested that the classical church visitors ensure that the catechism is being used seriously. Synod then added the stipulation that the "division to be preached [be] read to the congregation before the sermon is preached" (*Acts of Synod 1950*, p. 441).

5. Synod encouraged the churches also to use the Belgic Confession and the Canons of Dort in preaching (*Acts of Synod 1973*, p. 65).

THE MISSION AND EVANGELISM CHALLENGE

The Christian Reformed Church is a mission church. The denomination has carefully defined the mission challenge for the church at the local, classical, and synodical level. In doing so the denomination is responding to Christ's mandate: "Make disciples of all nations . . ." (Matt. 28:19; see also Mark 16:15-18; Luke 24:45-49; John 17:18; 20:21-23; Acts 1:8; 2 Cor. 5:18-21).

Lord's Day 21 of the Heidelberg Catechism states the challenge eloquently:

"I believe that the Son of God
through his Spirit and Word,
out of the entire human race,
from the beginning of the world to
its end,
gathers, protects, and preserves for
himself
a community chosen for eternal
life . . ."

In more recent times the church confessed in *Our World Belongs to God,* section 44:

"Following the apostles, the
church is sent—
sent with the gospel of the
kingdom
to make disciples of all nations,
to feed the hungry,

and to proclaim the assurance that
in the name of Christ
there is forgiveness of sin and new
life
for all who repent and believe—
to tell the news that our world
belongs to God."

In articles 73-77 of the Church Order the denomination spells out a number of basic provisions, giving this vision flesh and blood.

Councils have an important responsibility in leading their churches to obey the Great Commission. The Church Order stipulates that "each council shall stimulate the members of the congregation to be witnesses for Christ in word and deed and to support the work of home and foreign missions by their interest, prayers, and gifts" (art. 73b) and that ministers and elders shall "engage in and promote the work of evangelism" (art. 12a). In the form for the Ordination of Elders and Deacons, leaders are challenged to "share with all the good news of salvation."

What can the elders do?

The practice of evangelism, if it is to be consistent and productive, must spring from the heart of your congregation. Have you and your people been gripped by the immeasurable riches of the salvation Christ came to bring? Have you seen the spiritual beauty of his body, which is the church?

In the words of the Nicene Creed, the church professes to "believe in one holy catholic and apostolic church." The church is "holy" because it is garbed in Christ's holiness; "catholic" because it spans the centuries and comprises all generations; and "apostolic" as it compels people to come in.

The Great Commission is the driving force of the New Testament church. Allow that force to carry your church. Evangelism thrives in the right climate. Seek the presence of the Holy Spirit as he infuses your members with a deep concern for the salvation of the lost.

Your council will spend much of its time dealing with the nitty-gritty of church life. It must do so responsibly, for the spiritual well-being of your membership depends on it. Remember, though, to see the big picture: your calling to be a light shining brightly on a hill. Articulate that vision. Discuss it. Think about it. Read about it. Pray about it. Hope for it.

There are a number of things elders can do to implement this vision:[1]

• Do some of your members bring friends or neighbors to church? Take note of it; welcome the guests; show your appreciation to those members. Can a follow-up visit be arranged?

• Pastors who are excited about evangelism deserve the backing of their elders. Offer to assist your pastor in evangelistic calling.

• Does your church have an active evangelism committee? Let the committee know of your support. Join in on some of the things they do. Encourage the committee to mobilize the entire church. See to it that evangelism is properly reflected in the church budget.

• Do your share to bring inspirational missionary and evangelism speakers to your church. They will greatly enrich and motivate your members.

• Be aware of members who evidence the spiritual gift of evangelism. Perhaps all they need is a gentle push from you to join the ranks of active witnesses for Christ.

• Encourage your fellow officebearers to work toward worship services that are permeated with a spirit of openness and warmth, where visitors sense that they are valued, respected, and understood.

• Have you recognized the importance of "relational evangelism" and "side-door ministries" (such as Coffee Break, Men's Life, self-help groups, and so on) through which people can become acquainted with the life of the church?

• Word and deed are two sides of the evangelism coin. Work with the deacons of your church in programs of relief and assistance that underscore the gospel message.

- Be ingenious in thinking of symbolic gestures. Some believers sat in a circle or a group prayer. One chair was intentionally left empty. "That chair," one member said, "will be occupied by a guest we bring next time."

- Does your church have a vision and mission statement? It may not be mentioned often, but carry it with you and read from it at opportune moments.

- Volunteer for specific evangelism projects, and encourage your fellow officebearers to do so.

- If your church employs an evangelism staff person, show him or her your support. Don't let that person become a lone evangelism worker.

- Is your area covered by the broadcast of The Back to God Hour? Perhaps your church can assist in making follow-up calls to people who have written BTGH. Does your congregation know the details of the BTGH broadcast in your area?

- Widen your evangelism horizon. Evangelism is more than saving souls. "Thy kingdom come," Jesus taught his church to pray. His kingdom is here, and it is also on the way. All power in heaven and on earth is his. Through his Word and Spirit, Christ transforms lives, communities, and segments of society. Your Christian faithfulness has great future. The fruits of all sorts of kingdom service may only be recognized in the coming age. Your church is an outpost of the kingdom!

The same holds true for evangelism around the world. The CRC has had a long love affair with world missions. As far back as 1910, synod actually listed half a dozen ways that local churches could support the cause of the worldwide spread of the gospel. Synod pointed to preaching and teaching as prime avenues to instill the missionary spirit in their members. Synod challenged each church to sponsor its own missionary and hold regular mission festivals. Synod also proposed that "systematic weekly offerings be taken for missions." Good advice! (*Acts of Synod 1910*, p. 24)

Note

1. Assistance and helpful materials can be obtained from the offices of both Home Missions and World Missions at 2850 Kalamazoo Ave. SE, Grand Rapids, MI 49560, and The Back to God Hour, 6555 West College Drive, Palos Heights, IL 60463. The address of the Canadian office for all three agencies is PO Box 5070, STN LCD 1, Burlington, ON L7R 3Y8.

PART 5

BEYOND THE LOCAL CHURCH

In the last part of this manual we will explore the larger context in which God has placed your church. What is your relationship to other churches of the denomination and, beyond that, with other expressions of the Christian faith in our world?

59

BEING PART OF CLASSIS

The classis is one of three assemblies of the church: the council of a congregation, the classis, and the synod (Church Order, art. 26). A classis consists of delegates from a group of about twenty churches located in a certain geographic area (art. 39). The Christian Reformed Church is composed of forty-seven classes.

Of what benefit is the classis? There are several. The church of Christ is broader than the local congregation. Through classis, congregations enjoy fellowship, encourage and help each other, and are mutually accountable.

The churches agreed that classes should confine their work to two areas: matters that the congregations have in common and matters that the local council cannot finish by itself (art. 28b). Churches of classis may, for instance, decide to open a chaplaincy ministry at a nearby university campus. (This project would be too big for one church.) Or a council may be faced with an internal conflict that it finds difficult to solve, so it turns to classis, which may appoint a task force to provide assistance. Or classis may be instrumental in establishing new churches.

Mutual accountability, which the churches of classis assume for each other, finds concrete expression in article 41 of the Church Order. The president of classis directs the six questions listed there to the delegates of the churches.

In order to understand the authority by which classis does its work, we must first go to the local church. The church has a council that governs with the authority of Christ. The Church Order calls it *original authority* (art. 27a). Classis and synod are expressions of the broader unity of the church. They do their ministry, each in its assigned domain, with the same authority as the local council— from Christ. The Church Order calls this *delegated authority* since these assemblies are composed of delegates (art. 27a). However, a classis has authority over a local council (art. 28b), just as synod has authority over classes (art. 27a&b).

Following are a few more details you may wish to note regarding your classis:

1. Each church delegates a minister and an elder to classis. When a church is "vacant," two elders are delegated (art. 40a). Newly ordained elders are encouraged to attend classis meetings as observers to get a feel for the work.

2. Classis elects its own president for the sessions of classis. Ministers may also rotate for this function, but no one shall be president twice in a row (art. 40c).

Classis also has a stated clerk and a treasurer. They continue their function even when a classis is not in session. Their duties are outlined in article 32.

3. Classis meetings are open to visitors, except when it meets in "executive session." Officebearers who are not delegates may be given an "advisory voice" (art. 40a).

4. Classis, as well as the local church, must be properly incorporated. Is your church properly incorporated? (*Acts of Synod 1963,* p. 51; *Acts of Synod 1997,* pp. 616-620)

5. The local council must provide its delegates to classis with proper credentials authorizing them to participate in the work of classis (art. 34).

6. Classis is a deliberative body (art. 34). Its members vote on matters after they have had the benefit of due deliberation, discussion, and debate. That's why councils do not bind their delegates to vote a certain way. It is, of course, a council's privilege to send a communication to classis explaining its position on an issue coming before classis.

7. When a council is unable to delegate an elder to classis, it may designate a deacon to attend instead. Classis, having heard the reasons, will vote to seat the deacon as a voting member.

8. The denomination feels so strongly about the church's calling in the areas of evangelism and mercy that it requires classes to have a classical home missions committee and a classical diaconal committee (art. 75).

9. The preparation of gifted young members for the ministry is important; classes must have a student fund to assist them (art. 21).

10. The business of classes, between meetings, is administered by the classical interim committee.

11. A congregation may transfer from one classis to another. One of the two classes must approve the request. Synod also has to give its approval.

12. Local churches, normally, also relate to synod through their classis. Overtures, appeals, and communications to synod are carefully considered by classis for its possible support and processing.

60

WELCOMING THE CHURCH VISITORS

It is a time-honored custom in the Christian Reformed Church: classis, once a year, sends a delegation of two office-bearers to visit with all the councils of the churches in the classis (art. 42).

On behalf of the other churches the visitors come to see how each church in the classis is doing. The visitors bring encouragement, speak words of advice and commendation, and take due note of God's blessings.

The Church Order outlines five main areas that should be covered in the visit (art. 42b). However, synods were so concerned about the substance of the visit that they drafted a broader set of questions for the church visitors to ask. As more issues arose, more questions were added. Now there are almost fifty questions.

The intention was noble, but church visitors are now often under much pressure to finish the visit in time. Moreover, formal questions tend to solicit formal answers. Many church visits have turned into a probing examination rather than a meeting of hearts. Perhaps you remember some visits that you found less than edifying. Church visiting as such, however, is a fine institution and deserves to be preserved.

Church visitors should take note of the questions, make a mental summary of the subjects, determine which apply to the council they are to visit, and cover the material briefly with the council members. The focus of the visit should be on the well-being of the church and its council. The council should set the agenda. Its members should tell of struggles, disappointments, and setbacks, but also of progress, victories, and growth. In response, the church visitors will listen, empathize, encourage, and advise. They will lead in meaningful prayer. This can only happen when the local officebearers make the visit a matter of prayer and reflect carefully on what they wish to report to the church visitors (*Acts of Synod 1936*, pp. 122-123).

Some other details:

1. Classis may send two ministers or one minister and one elder. Synod said that the visitors have to be "experienced and competent officebearers" (art. 42a). Most classes appoint two or more teams.

2. Synod said that the visit should be made once a year (art. 42a). In some classes the visits are made only once every two or three years. If these visits are to be truly helpful, the councils should probably insist on an annual visit

(*Acts of Synod 1975,* p. 17). The upcoming visit should be announced to all council members and the congregation.

3. Councils may also invite the church visitors to come in whenever serious problems arise (art. 42c).

4. The church visitors submit a written report of their work to classis (art. 42d).

61

BEING PART OF SYNOD

Chances are good that some of your elders have attended synod. They will probably remember it as a demanding but rewarding experience. Synod is not only a deliberative body, it is also an occasion for learning a lot.

Articles 45-50 of the Church Order outline the structure and function of synod.

Synod is composed of four delegates from each classis—two ministers and two elders. They represent the churches of their classis (art. 45). Synod meets once a year (art. 46a). Each synod designates a church to convene the following synod (art. 46a). Synod elects four officers—a president, a vice president, a first clerk, and a second clerk. The first meeting of synod precedes a prayer service which is held the day after the convening session. Most classes are prepared to compensate elder delegates for loss of wages when needed. A program committee, composed of the officers of the previous synod, drafts the agenda of an upcoming synod. The program committee also appoints the advisory committees from the list of delegates well before the actual meeting of synod and assigns agenda material to each. This facilitates the preparation that delegates must make for the meetings. The denomination's general secretary, the executive director of ministries, the director of finance, the presidents of Calvin College and Seminary, and the seminary professors serve as functionaries and advisers of synod.

What do synods do?

Synods deal with matters that concern the churches in common and matters that the classes cannot finish (art. 28b). The Church Order outlines six areas in which synod does basic work: adoption of creeds, Church Order, liturgical forms, *Psalter Hymnal*, principles and elements of the order of worship, and Bible versions (art. 47).

Synod also supervises a variety of denominational ministries: Home Missions, World Missions, The Back to God Hour, Christian Reformed World Relief, Calvin College, Calvin Seminary, CRC Publications, Ministers' Pension Funds, Fund for Smaller Churches, World Literature Ministries, Pastoral Ministries (Race Relations, Chaplaincy Ministries, Disability Concerns, Pastor-Church Relations, and Abuse Prevention) and others. Synod is assisted in the work of supervision by the denominational Board of Trustees.

In order to facilitate its work, synod often appoints study committees, which may take two or more years to work on their assignments. Synod's overall responsibilities are also aided by several permanent "service committees" (previously called "standing committees").

Annually, synod sets the amount that the churches are asked to contribute toward the denominational ministries. They are called "ministry shares" (previously called "quotas").

By what authority does synod do its work? The Church Order gives the following summary: "Each assembly exercises . . . the ecclesiastical authority entrusted to the church by Christ; the authority of councils being original, that of major assemblies being delegated." Also, "the classis has the same authority over the council as the synod has over the classis" (art. 27). (See also section |53.) That's why the work of synods should be respected and appreciated. Synod has rightly noted that movements and actions that undermine the authori-

---

To what extent are officebearers bound by synodical pronouncements and actions?
Synodical "deliverances" are not at the same authority level as the confessions of the church. Still, article 29 of the Church Order states that they are "considered settled and binding, unless it is proved that they conflict with the Word of God or the Church Order."

A denomination cannot hope to function fruitfully if common agreements are ignored at will. That does not mean that individual officebearers cannot feel unhappy with certain synodical expressions or actions.

Keep in mind that synodical deliverances stem from a large variety of problems, needs, opportunities, and situations. When synod interprets a creedal statement, adherence is much more consequential than an instance of synodical, pastoral advice. Synod once pointed out that each synodical decision has its own "use and function," which is clearly reflected by the very wording of each decision (e.g., pronouncements about creeds,

expressions of the faith, adjudications, testimonies, guidelines for ministries and actions, pastoral advice, organizational regulations, etc.). The weight and consequences of an officebearer's disagreement are affected by all these situational nuances (*Acts of Synod 1975*, pp. 44-46).

Church leaders will, however, always be aware that the responsibilities and privileges of their offices necessitate a healthy respect for synodical deliverances. The church, therefore, has always expected her officebearers not to express their differences in teaching and writing, nor to agitate for noncompliance.

An interesting example may be found in the synodical pronouncements on keeping the Lord's Day. Synod of 1881 adopted six guidelines for the observation of the Lord's Day (*Acts of Synod 1881*, p. 19). Synod of 1926 affirmed the "Six Points of 1881" and added that they should be accepted as "an interpretation of the confessional writings . . . therefore, binding for every officer and member" (*Acts of Synod 1926*, pp. 191-192).

ty of assemblies—be they council, classis, or synod—bring great harm to the unity of the church (*Acts of Synod 1991,* pp. 812-814).

Be reminded that the synodical office is a ready source of assistance and advice for local councils: General Secretary, 2850 Kalamazoo Ave. SE, Grand Rapids, MI 49560. Phone (616) 224-0744. E-mail engelhad@crcna.org

BEING PART OF THE WORLDWIDE CHURCH

We are thankful for the Christian Reformed Church and the Reformed faith. We are equally thankful for the multitude of Christian churches around the world that form with us the worldwide church of Christ. God promised Abraham that in his seed, Jesus Christ, all nations would be blessed. Where that unity of all believers becomes visible, we rejoice.

The Belgic Confession speaks of that vision eloquently:

"And so this holy church
is not confined,
bound,
or limited to a certain place or
    certain persons.
But is spread and dispersed
throughout the entire world,
though still joined and united
in heart and will,
in one and the same Spirit
by the power of faith." *(art. 27)*

In 1987 our denomination adopted the first version of the Ecumenical Charter in which the vision of the worldwide body of believers is spelled out and the possibilities of practicing fellowship and cooperation with other Christian church bodies are rehearsed (art. 49; *Acts of Synod 1985,* pp. 205, 237-241; *Acts of Synod 1987,* pp. 587-591; *Acts of Synod 1988,* pp. 562-564).

With an appeal to John 17, 1 Corinthians 12, and Ephesians 4, and Lord's Day 21 of the Heidelberg Catechism, the Charter states that biblical truth must be cherished but that unity itself is also an expression of truth and a gift of Christ. "The unity of the church must become visibly manifest. The ideal form of such unity is not yet known. We therefore earnestly seek the leading of the Holy Spirit into a unity which is one of mutual renewal and acceptance," the Charter states.

The Christian Reformed Church has taken some concrete steps toward biblical ecumenism. Although these steps are modest when viewed against the task of worldwide evangelization, they are steps of which we can be rightly proud.

Biblical ecumenical efforts have taken place through many years in many places, as many individual CRC congregations cooperated with other Christian groups. Increased goodwill and respect were often the result.

On a denominational level, the ecumenical effort was mainly sustained by synod's Interchurch Relations Committee (IRC). For many years this committee has established various forms of contact and cooperation with denominations whose confessions differed little from the CRC's. It has also made promising contacts with broader evangelical communities. In addition, the IRC has established imaginative relationships with the worldwide community of Reformed churches, many of them designated by synod as "churches in ecclesiastical fellowship." With them we exchange fraternal delegates at major assemblies, enjoy pulpit fellowship, share in communion around the Lord's table, join in common actions, and communicate on issues of joint concern. These denominations are found not only on this continent but in countries in Latin America, Asia, Europe, Africa, and Australia.

The CRC is also in contact with several Christian denominations with whom we are exploring cooperation. They are known as "Churches in Corresponding Fellowship" (*Acts of Synod 1993*, pp. 408-410, 504).

Our denomination also belongs to several ecumenical organizations under whose umbrella we remain in contact and engage in common action with various denominations:

- The *Reformed Ecumenical Council* (REC), with headquarters at 2050 Breton Rd. SE, Suite 102, Grand Rapids, MI 49546, comprises numerous Reformed church groups from around the world. The REC is a significant platform for the advancement of Reformed faith and action.

- The *National Association of Evangelicals* (NAE) has enabled the CRC to interact with a broad segment of the American evangelical church world. The NAE has been very congenial to CRC input.

- Mention should be made of the efforts of the Canadian segment of the CRC through its *Council of the Christian Reformed Churches in Canada* (CCRCC). During the last three decades, it has established a large number of constructive contacts with Canadian church organizations. One important avenue was its membership in the *Evangelical Fellowship of Canada* (EFC) in which CRC people assumed positions of leadership. The council also joined the *Canada Council of Churches*. These liaisons have enabled the CRC in Canada to express a strong Christian testimony in societal matters. In 1998 the CCRCC was disbanded and its responsibilities assumed by the Canadian Ministries Board of the CRC Board of Trustees.

All churches, including the CRC, must come to a clearer understanding of God's truth as revealed in the Word so that barriers against unity may dissolve. That means that we must not only testify but also listen. True dialogue comprises both speaking and hearing. Many churches with which we dialogue have gone through fierce persecution. We can learn much from them. Many churches are located in regions of abject poverty. Others have penetrated a hostile environment with the gospel. They too can teach us.

The beauty of ecumenism is that it opens our eyes to the great things Christ is doing in incredibly diversified settings, that it makes the unity we have with fellow believers around the world increasingly visible, and that we grow in appreciation for the treasures we possess in our local churches. This has also been expressed by the services the CCRCC has rendered through cooperation with the Interchurch Committee on Human Rights in Latin America, the Aboriginal Rights Coalition, and the Committee on Refugees.

IN SUPPORT OF CHRISTIAN SCHOOLS

The CRC has always been committed to Christian day school education.[1] Christian leaders from previous generations saw to it that leaders today would share the same commitment. "The council shall diligently encourage the members of the congregation to establish and maintain good Christian schools . . ." (Church Order, art. 71). Synods through the years confirmed that challenge by saying that our children are religious beings whose needs are foremost spiritual, and whose commitment must be to the truth

- that education is the nurturing of the whole person in the fear of God which is the beginning of wisdom.
- that baptism is the sign of the covenant and that Christian education is part of covenantal living.
- that life knows of no separation between the sacred and the secular and that Christian education honors our King, who has been given dominion over all life's realms. (*Acts of Synod 1898*, p. 38; *Acts of Synod 1951*, p. 44; *Acts of Synod 1955*, pp. 193-200; see also *Our World Belongs to God*, section 50.)

What can councils do?

1. Keep the issue of Christian day school education before the congregation. The Church Order uses the word "encourage." In an edifying way let your members know that Christian education is dear to you as spiritual leaders. Pastors deserve the elders' support when they express the vision from the pulpit. There may be some elders who feel unable to send their children to a Christian school. Their support for Christian education should still be earnestly solicited.

2. On a personal basis, encourage Christian school teachers in your church circles. Show your interest in their work and well-being. And don't forget the Christian school board members. All these people must fulfill an awesome task with limited means. Stop by your nearby schools now and then. Attend Christian school events, even when you have no children in school. Encourage Christian teachers and administrators in public schools to express a Christian testimony in their schools.

3. As a council, ensure that your church has funds available for parents who lack sufficient financial resources to meet tuition costs. Encourage all your members to give their financial support.

Note

1. Contact Christian Schools International, 3350 East Paris Ave., PO Box 8709, Grand Rapids, MI 49508 for helpful advice and resources.

RELATING TO PARACHURCH ORGANIZATIONS

Religious life in Canada and the U.S. is flanked by scores of religious and charitable organizations and advocacy groups, each struggling for a niche in which to do their work. Local church councils are regularly approached by these organizations for financial support and sometimes for endorsement.

It is not easy for councils to define a set of guidelines to assist them in making responsible and intelligent choices.

Here are observations that may serve you:

1. Synods have pointed out regularly that the denomination's own ministries ought to have the churches' priority when requests for aid are considered. Among them are ministries in the area of evangelism, missions, mercy, and education, whose programs are only partially supported by ministry shares. Every year synod lists these causes in the *Acts of Synod* and sends lists to the church treasurers. Synod recommends these causes for "one or more offerings." Synod adds a special list for some youth causes.

2. Synods have also maintained contact with scores of nondenominational organizations and have recommended them to the churches for support. Their names are also listed in the *Acts of Synod* under three headings: benevolent agencies, educational agencies, and miscellaneous agencies. Separate lists are drawn up for the U.S. and Canada.

The organizations listed there submit full reports of their ministries and financial dealings to synod, and are annually reviewed by synod's Board of Trustees. Since more than forty organizations are mentioned, local churches have plenty of choices. You can be confident that your gift is put to good use by any of these organizations. You may not have that certainty with organizations not mentioned on synod's list.

3. There are many organizations that are active in areas not mentioned on synod's list. If you feel deeply about their mission and feel inclined to support them, by all means check them out. Ask them to send you their annual report, their budget, and their financial report, and ask specifically which part of your support dollar goes for promotion, administration, and actual ministry.

4. You will probably be approached by local causes. Your council members may know something about the values and ministry of these organizations. But it's appropriate to do some research as well. You may conclude that these causes merit your support since they meet

needs in an area of interest to you. Life would be unlivable for many people across the continent without such organizations.

Since available support funds are limited, you may wish to give the denominational causes and causes related to the denomination your top priority.

On the other hand, we are grateful that in this broken and needy world there are many organizations that do great work and bring solace and relief to those who suffer terribly. Follow the dictates of your heart, but also follow your head: can it be demonstrated that recommending them for support is warranted? If so, do it wholeheartedly. This is a true saying: churches that give generously to a variety of causes have less trouble making their local budget.

IN CONCLUSION: GODSPEED

"Of making many books there is no end, and much study wearies the body" (Eccles. 12:12).

Must you go by the book as you work as an elder? I would not answer that question with a resounding "yes." You are called, foremost, to be a shepherd. You have a shepherd's heart. In the company of the great Shepherd, follow his dictates.

Church life comes with so many unpredictable situations, so many problems for which there are no solutions, so much pain for which there seems to be no solace. On many occasions you find yourself improvising, but amid the complexities of congregational realities you will be able to find some guideposts on the preceding pages.

Elders of generations long ago had experiences similar to yours. Much of ecclesiastical literature and usage reflects their wisdom. Perhaps in pastoral caregiving, reinventing the wheel can be avoided.

"May the God of peace, who through the blood of the eternal covenant brought back from the dead our Lord Jesus, that great Shepherd of the sheep, equip you with everything good for doing his will, and may he work in us what is pleasing to him, through Jesus Christ, to whom be glory for ever and ever, Amen."
—Hebrews 13:20-21

BIBLIOGRAPHY

Arnold, Harry G. *Discipline in the Church* (number 14 in the series *In His Service*). Grand Rapids, Mich.: CRC Publications, 1989.

Berghoef, Gerard, and Lester DeKoster. *The Elder's Handbook*. Grand Rapids, Mich.: Christian Library Press, 1979.

Church Order/Rules for Synodical Procedure. Grand Rapids, Mich.: CRC Publications, 1997.

De Jong, James A. *Into His Presence*. Grand Rapids, Mich.: CRC Publications, 1985.

De Jong, Peter Y. *Taking Heed of the Flock*. Grand Rapids, Mich.: Baker Book House, 1955.

De Koning, Neil. *Guiding the Faith Journey: A Map For Spiritual Leaders*. Grand Rapids, Mich.: CRC Publications, 1996.

De Ridder, Richard R. *Organization of the Church; The Place and Function of Members; The Special Offices of the Church; Family Visitation* (numbers 2, 3, 4, and 8 in the series *In His Service*). Grand Rapids, Mich.: CRC Publications.

Foster, Richard. *Celebration of Discipline: The Path to Spiritual Growth*. New York: Harper and Row, 1978.

Guenther, Margaret. *Holy Listening: The Art of Spiritual Direction*. Boston: Cowley Publishing, 1992.

Kooistra, Remkes. *Straight Talk: A Fresh Look at 1 Timothy*. Grand Rapids, Mich.: CRC Publications, 1996.

Oates, Wayne E. *A Practical Handbook for Ministry*. Louisville: Westminster/John Knox Press, 1992.

Postema, Don. *Space for God: Study and Practice of Spirituality and Prayer*. 2nd ed. Grand Rapids, Mich.: CRC Publications, 1997.

Tamminga, Louis. *Conflict in the Church* (number 12 in the series *In His Service*). Grand Rapids, Mich.: CRC Publications.

————. *A New Pastor for Greensville*. Grand Rapids, Mich.: CRC Pastor-Church Relations, 1988.

Vander Griend, Alvin J. *Discover Your Gifts*. 2nd ed. Grand Rapids, Mich.: CRC Publications, 1997.

TOPICAL INDEX

TOPICAL INDEX